The Lion book of

CLASSIC BIBLE PASSAGES

ONE HUNDRED SELECTED QUOTATIONS
– FROM GENESIS TO REVELATION

COMPILED BY
TIMOTHY DUDLEY-SMITH

A LION BOOK
Oxford . Batavia . Sydney

Copyright © 1989 Timothy Dudley-Smith

Published by
Lion Publishing plc
Sandy Lane West, Littlemore, Oxford, England
ISBN 0 7459 1540 X
Lion Publishing Corporation
1705 Hubbard Avenue, Batavia, Illinois 60510, USA
ISBN 0 7459 1540 X
Albatross Books Pty Ltd
PO Box 320, Sutherland, NSW 2232, Australia
ISBN 0 7324 0018 X

First edition 1989

Acknowledgments
Bible quotations are used by kind permission of the following:
Authorized King James Version of the Bible, 1662, Crown copyright
Good News Bible, copyright 1966, 1971 and 1976 American Bible Society, published by the Bible Societies/Collins
Jerusalem Bible, copyright 1966, 1967 and 1968 Darton, Longman & Todd Ltd and Doubleday & Company Inc.
The New Testament in Modern English, copyright 1960 J.B. Phillips
The New English Bible, second edition, copyright 1970 Oxford and Cambridge University Presses
Holy Bible, New International Version (British edition), copyright 1978 New York International Bible Society
Revised Standard Version, copyright 1946 and 1952, second edition 1971, Division of Christian Education, National Council of the Churches of Christ in the USA

Photographs
Howard Barlow page 72; Susannah Burton pages 25, 36–37, 90–91, 114–15, 118–19; Hutchison Picture Library pages 14–15, 85; Frank Lane page 47; Sonia Halliday and Laura Lushington Photographs pages 38–39, 64–65, 76–77, 88–89, 100, 105 /Jane Taylor pages 20–21, 55, 67 /the late F.H.C. Birch pages 12–13; Lion Publishing/David Alexander pages 17, 58–59, 63, 80–81, 98–99, 126–27 /David Townsend pages 19, 28–29, 32–33, 34–35, 42–43, 44, 56, 68–69, 75, 78–79, 102–103 /Jon Willcocks page 116; Mansell Collection page 112; Alistair Duncan pages 52–53; David Townsend Photography pages 48–49, 110–11; ZEFA (UK) Ltd cover, pages 6, 8, 10–11, 50, 70, 87, 94–95, 120–21

British Library Cataloguing in Publication Data

Bible. English. Selections. 1989.
  The Lion book of classic Bible passages: one hundred selected quotations, from Genesis to Revelation/ compiled by Timothy Dudley-Smith. — 1st ed.
     p.   cm.
    ISBN 0–7459–1540–X
    I. Dudley-Smith, Timothy. II. Title. III. Title: Classic Bible passages.
BS391.2.D85 1989
220.5'2—dc19

Printed in Italy

THE TRANSLATIONS

KJV	Authorized King James Version
GNB	Good News Bible
JB	Jerusalem Bible
JBP	J.B. Phillips' translation (of the whole New Testament, and later of selected parts of the Old)
NEB	New English Bible
NIV	New International Version
RSV	Revised Standard Version

CONTENTS

FOREWORD

This book is not the Bible, but only chosen excerpts from it. In compiling it, I have thought of it as a string of pearls. Each of these extracts is different: some are history, some prophecy, some from the Gospels, some from the New Testament letters. Some are 'larger' than others, not only in the sense of being longer on the page, but of dealing with bigger and weightier themes. Each one is precious. But they are not like a hundred pearls loose in a box, for I have followed almost exactly the Bible order (with one or two small exceptions), and there is therefore a progression in these pages. They scan the whole Bible, from the first chapter almost to the last, and form an outline introduction to its story and its major themes. In that sense, this book can be said to be like pearls arranged in order on a necklace.

These hundred short passages represent the main divisions of the Bible: thirty-five are from the Old Testament, thirty-five from the four Gospels (some from each, but most from Luke), and thirty from the remainder of the New Testament. Of these, nine are from the Acts of the Apostles, four from the Book of Revelation, and the rest from the New Testament letters or 'Epistles'.

In the space available less than half the books of the Old Testament are represented. Gideon and Samson, Ruth and Esther, Ezra and Nehemiah, Jonah and his great fish — you will find none of these. In the New Testament we fare better with seventeen out of its twenty-seven books having at least one passage included. But if you run your eye down the list of contents you will see, in broadest outline, the sweep of the history of Israel, the life of Jesus, and the beginnings of the Christian church.

The extracts from the Bible are taken from a variety of translations, some old and some new. I have tried to choose the most suitable of these translations, so as to convey both the meaning and the 'feeling' of a given passage. One or two, therefore, are in the familiar words on which older readers may have been brought up; but others are in more direct and contemporary language. Readers will be able to judge for themselves which kind of translation they find more satisfying.

There are many ways of attending to what the Bible is about, and I hope this book will help with some of them. The Bible uses vivid images to describe itself. It is like a lamp, giving us light to find our way in darkness and difficulty. It is a mirror held up to human nature, which helps us see ourselves. It is like honey, nourishing and full of sweetness — but also like a hammer, pounding relentlessly at the hard of heart. Perhaps this book is not only a string of pearls, but also a packet of seeds — for the words of Scripture are like seeds sown in our hearts, as Jesus described in his parable of the different soils. Through these words the living God makes himself known to us and speaks to us today.

My hope is that those who use this book as a beginning may go on to read the Bible for themselves. For that, there is no substitute.

TIMOTHY DUDLEY-SMITH

IN THE BEGINNING

Both the Old and the New Testaments start with the same words, 'In the beginning...' Their message is that before all else began to be, God was there, from eternity to eternity. No explanation is given of him, since it is the purpose of the Bible to reveal him. In its pages he makes himself known to us his creatures.

This story of the creation is cast in a more profound language than that of scientific description or understanding. It is the work of a mystic, an inspired thinker, a poet; and it offers us the truths of God's creative acts in these terms. Science and human discovery have been described as 'thinking God's thoughts after him'; but in this passage we are taken behind the means and mechanisms, and given a glimpse of the great purposes of God in human history. We begin here with the formless void, the dark abyss, and the mighty wind of God's creative Spirit.

In the beginning of creation, when God made heaven and earth, the earth was without form and void, with darkness over the face of the abyss, and a mighty wind that swept over the surface of the waters. God said, 'Let there be light,' and there was light; and God saw that the light was good, and he separated light from darkness. He called the light day, and the darkness night. So evening came, and morning came, the first day.

God said, 'Let there be a vault between the waters, to separate water from water.' So God made the vault, and separated the water under the vault from the water above it, and so it was; and God called the vault heaven. Evening came, and morning came, a second day.

God said, 'Let the waters under heaven be gathered into one place, so that dry land may appear'; and so it was. 'God called the dry land earth, and the gathering of the waters he called seas; and God saw that it was good. Then God said, 'Let the earth produce fresh growth, let there be on the earth plants bearing seed, fruit-trees bearing fruit each with seed according to its kind.' So it was; the earth yielded fresh growth, plants bearing seed according to their kind and trees bearing fruit each with seed according to its kind; and God saw that it was good. Evening came, and morning came, a third day.

God said, 'Let there be lights in the vault of heaven to separate day from night, and let them serve as signs both for festivals and for seasons and years. Let them also shine in the vault of heaven to give light on earth.' So it was; God made the two great lights, the greater to govern the day and the lesser to govern the night; and with them he made the stars. God put these lights in the vault of heaven to give light on earth, to govern day and night, and to separate light from darkness; and God saw that it was good. Evening came, and morning came, a fourth day.

God said, 'Let the waters teem with countless living creatures, and let birds fly above the earth across the vault of heaven.' God then created the great sea-monsters and all living creatures that move and swarm in the waters, according to their kind, and every kind of bird; and God saw that it was good. So he blessed them and said, 'Be fruitful and increase, fill the waters of the seas; and let the birds increase on land.' Evening came, and morning came, a fifth day.

God said, 'Let the earth bring forth living creatures, according to their kind: cattle, reptiles, and wild animals, all according to their kind.' So it was; God made wild animals, cattle, and all reptiles, each according to its kind; and he saw that it was good.

GENESIS 1:1-26 *NEB*

2

God is love. At the heart of his creation there were to be persons whom he loved, and who would respond by loving him in return. We are these persons, young and old, male and female, black and white, made 'in the image of God'. We bear within us, however blurred or defaced, the likeness of the God who made us.

We are the crown of God's creation. The earth is ours to tend and care for, to be our home. Man is God's vice-regent, to rule his world — a world which, as it left its Maker's hands, was 'very good'. And so God rested, with the work of creation finished; and because we are made in his image, he gives to us also patterns of day and night, light and darkness, work and rest.

Then God said, 'Let us make man in our image and likeness to rule the fish in the sea, the birds of heaven, the cattle, all wild animals on earth, and all reptiles that crawl upon the earth.' So God created man in his own image; in the image of God he created him; male and female he created them. God blessed them and said to them, 'Be fruitful and increase, fill the earth and subdue it, rule over the fish in the sea, the birds of heaven, and every living thing that moves upon the earth.' God also said, 'I give you all plants that bear seed everywhere on earth, and every tree bearing fruit which yields seed: they shall be yours for food. All green plants I give for food to the wild animals, to all the birds of heaven, and to all reptiles on earth, every living creature.' So it was; and God saw all that he had made, and it was very good. Evening came, and morning came, a sixth day.

Thus heaven and earth were completed with all their mighty throng. On the sixth day God completed all the work he had been doing, and on the seventh day he ceased from all his work. God blessed the seventh day and made it holy, because on that day he ceased from all the work he had set himself to do.

This is the story of the making of heaven and earth when they were created.

GENESIS 1:27 — 2:4 *NEB*

3

GOOD AND EVIL

The opening chapters of the Bible show us the divine origin of much that we take for granted in our life today. The alternation of work and rest; human partnership, sexuality and marriage; the separation of the fully human from the animal creation; the spiritual nature of men and women as made in the image of the divine — all these and more are in this deceptively simple story. But if that were all, it would bear little relation to the world we live in as our newspapers daily describe it.

Genesis chapter 3 gives us the Bible's account of how evil crept into our world from the beginning. If God's creatures were to be truly human they must be free to choose evil as well as good; to disobey as well as to obey: for without freedom there can be no love. So, in less than a chapter, the story speaks to us of the coming of temptation, the lure of the forbidden and the subtlety with which it presents itself to us. Sin, guilt, shame and death come to us as the legacy of our first parents — and from this chapter comes also the sense of God's unremitting love for fallen creatures, and his plan for our final restoration. This is the story of all the Scriptures, which finds its fulfilment in the coming of Christ.

Now the serpent was more crafty than any of the wild animals the Lord God had made. He said to the woman, 'Did God really say, "You must not eat from any tree in the garden"?'

The woman said to the serpent, 'We may eat fruit from the trees in the garden, but God did say, "You must not eat fruit from the tree that is in the middle of the garden, and you must not touch it, or you will die."'

'You will not surely die,' the serpent said to the woman. 'For God knows that when you eat of it your eyes will be opened, and you will be like God, knowing good and evil.'

When the woman saw that the fruit of the tree was good for food and pleasing to the eye, and also desirable for gaining wisdom, she took some and ate it. She also gave some to her husband, who was with her, and he ate it. Then the eyes of both of them were opened, and they realised that they were naked; so they sewed fig leaves together and made coverings for themselves.

Then the man and his wife heard the sound of the Lord God as he was walking in the garden in the cool of the day, and they hid from the Lord God among the trees of the garden. But the Lord God called to the man, 'Where are you?'

He answered, 'I heard you in the garden, and I was afraid because I was naked; so I hid.'

And he said, 'Who told you that you were naked? Have you eaten from the tree from which I commanded you not to eat?'

The man said, 'The woman you put here with me — she gave me some fruit from the tree, and I ate it.'

Then the Lord God said to the woman, 'What is this you have done?'

The woman said, 'The serpent deceived me, and I ate.'

GENESIS 3:1-13 *NIV*

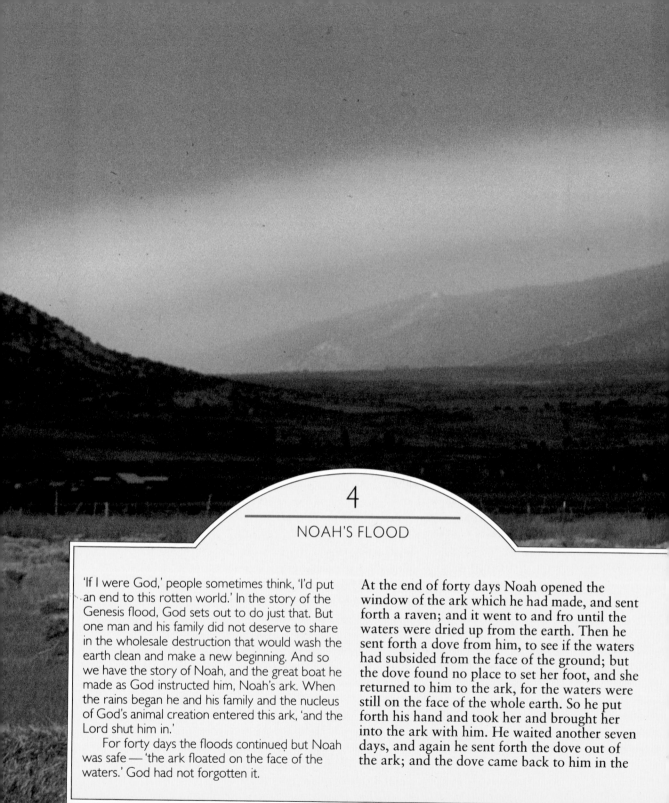

4

NOAH'S FLOOD

'If I were God,' people sometimes think, 'I'd put an end to this rotten world.' In the story of the Genesis flood, God sets out to do just that. But one man and his family did not deserve to share in the wholesale destruction that would wash the earth clean and make a new beginning. And so we have the story of Noah, and the great boat he made as God instructed him, Noah's ark. When the rains began he and his family and the nucleus of God's animal creation entered this ark, 'and the Lord shut him in.'

For forty days the floods continued but Noah was safe — 'the ark floated on the face of the waters.' God had not forgotten it.

At the end of forty days Noah opened the window of the ark which he had made, and sent forth a raven; and it went to and fro until the waters were dried up from the earth. Then he sent forth a dove from him, to see if the waters had subsided from the face of the ground; but the dove found no place to set her foot, and she returned to him to the ark, for the waters were still on the face of the whole earth. So he put forth his hand and took her and brought her into the ark with him. He waited another seven days, and again he sent forth the dove out of the ark; and the dove came back to him in the

evening, and lo, in her mouth a freshly plucked olive leaf; so Noah knew that the waters had subsided from the earth. Then he waited another seven days, and sent forth the dove; and she did not return to him any more.

In the six hundred and first year, in the first month, the first day of the month, the waters were dried from off the earth; and Noah removed the covering of the ark, and looked, and behold, the face of the ground was dry.

GENESIS 8:6-13 *RSV*

So begins a new relationship between God and his creation. God enters into an agreement, or covenant, never again to destroy the world by flood; and he marks this covenant by a sign, the rainbow, a reminder in a watery world of what he has promised. And with the rainbow there comes also his divine assurance, that 'while the earth remains, seedtime and harvest, cold and heat, summer and winter, day and night, shall not cease.'

GOD'S COVENANT WITH ABRAHAM

Abraham, whose name began as Abram, is depicted throughout the Bible as the man of faith. God spoke to him, and he believed God, and obeyed him. Because of this, God promised him a land in which to settle, and called him to be the founder of the chosen people. Through his descendants in the fulness of time God would work out his purpose for the deliverance of all mankind. So God makes a covenant with Abraham, more personal and far-reaching than his covenant with Noah; and it is in the fulfilment of this covenant-relationship that Christ was born.

Abraham and his wife Sarah were old and had no children of their own. Here, according to his faith, God promises that they will have a son, the founder of a great nation, a nation who would fulfil his divine purpose as the people of God.

The word of the Lord came to Abram in a vision, 'Fear not, Abram, I am your shield; your reward shall be very great.' But Abram said, 'O Lord God, what wilt thou give me, for I continue childless, and the heir of my house is Eliezer of Damascus?' And Abram said, 'Behold, thou hast given me no offspring; and a slave born in my house will be my heir.' And behold, the word of the Lord came to him, 'This man shall not be your heir; your own son shall be your heir.' And he brought him outside and said, 'Look toward heaven, and number the stars, if you are able to number them.' Then he said to him, 'So shall your descendants be.' And he believed the Lord; and he reckoned it to him as righteousness.

GENESIS 15:1-6 *RSV*

6

ABRAHAM'S FAITH

Sarah gives birth to a son and they call him Isaac. When God later commands Abraham to sacrifice his son, it seems not only contrary to natural affection but, to all human reckoning, a denial of God's promises already made to him and so a frustration of the divine purpose. Yet, in faith, he prepared to obey even where he could not understand.

After these things God tested Abraham, and said to him, 'Abraham!' And he said, 'Here am I.' He said, 'Take your son, your only son Isaac, whom you love, and go to the land of Moriah, and offer him there as a burnt offering upon one of the mountains of which I shall tell you.' So Abraham rose early in the morning, saddled his ass, and took two of his young men with him, and his son Isaac; and he cut the wood for the burnt offering, and arose and went to the place of which God had told him. On the third day Abraham lifted up his eyes and saw the place afar off. Then Abraham said to his young men, 'Stay here with the ass; I and the lad will go yonder and worship, and come again to you.' And Abraham took the wood of the burnt offering, and laid it on Isaac his son; and he took in his hand the fire and the knife. So they went both of them together. And Isaac said to his father Abraham, 'My father!' And he said, 'Here am I, my son.' He said, 'Behold, the fire and the wood; but where is the lamb for a burnt offering?' Abraham said, 'God will provide himself the lamb for a burnt offering, my son.' So they went both of them together.

When they came to the place of which God had told him, Abraham built an altar there, and laid the wood in order, and bound Isaac his son, and laid him on the altar, upon the wood. Then Abraham put forth his hand, and took the knife to slay his son. But the angel of the Lord called to him from heaven, and said, 'Abraham, Abraham!' And he said, 'Here am I.' He said, 'Do not lay your hand on the lad or do anything to him; for now I know that you fear God, seeing you have not withheld your son, your only son, from me.' And Abraham lifted up his eyes and looked, and behold, behind him was a ram, caught in a thicket by his horns; and Abraham went and took the ram, and offered it up as a burnt offering instead of his son. So Abraham called the name of that place The Lord will provide; as it is said to this day, 'On the mount of the Lord it shall be provided.'

GENESIS 22:1-14 *RSV*

7

JOSEPH, THE DREAMER

Jacob was grandson to Abraham, the man of faith and father of the covenant. Joseph, the youngest of Jacob's large family, was his father's favourite. He dreamed that one day his whole family would bow down to him.

Jacob loved Joseph more than all his other sons, because he had been born to him when he was old. He made a long robe with full sleeves for him. When his brothers saw that their father loved Joseph more than he loved them, they hated their brother so much that they would not speak to him in a friendly manner . . .

One day when Joseph's brothers had gone to Shechem to take care of their father's flock, Jacob said to Joseph, 'I want you to go to Shechem, where your brothers are taking care of the flock.'

Joseph answered, 'I am ready.'

His father said, 'Go and see if your brothers are safe and if the flock is all right; then come back and tell me.' So his father sent him on his way from the Valley of Hebron.

Joseph arrived at Shechem and was wandering about in the country when a man saw him and asked him, 'What are you looking for?'

'I am looking for my brothers, who are taking care of their flock,' he answered. 'Can you tell me where they are?'

The man said, 'They have already left. I heard them say that they were going to Dothan.' So Joseph went after his brothers and found them at Dothan.

They saw him in the distance, and before he reached them, they plotted against him and decided to kill him. They said to one another, 'Here comes that dreamer. Come on now, let's kill him and throw his body into one of the dry wells. We can say that a wild animal killed him. Then we will see what becomes of his dreams.'

Reuben heard them and tried to save Joseph. 'Let's not kill him,' he said. 'Just throw him into this well in the wilderness, but don't hurt him.' He said this, planning to save him from them and send him back to his father. When Joseph came up to his brothers, they ripped off his long robe with full sleeves. Then they took him and threw him into the well, which was dry.

While they were eating, they suddenly saw a group of Ishmaelites travelling from Gilead to Egypt. Their camels were loaded with spices and resins. Judah said to his brothers, 'What will we gain by killing our brother and covering up the

murder? Let's sell him to these Ishmaelites. Then we won't have to hurt him; after all, he is our brother, our own flesh and blood.' His brothers agreed, and when some Midianite traders came by, the brothers pulled Joseph out of the well and sold him for twenty pieces of silver to the Ishmaelites, who took him to Egypt.

GENESIS 37:3-4,12-28 *GNB*

Joseph's story has been summed up as 'a spoilt boy sold into Egyptian slavery by jealous brothers, who makes good in adversity and from an unjust imprisonment rises to the highest offices of state'. It was through Joseph that the tribe of Abraham would come to find themselves exiles in the land of Egypt. The experience of exile becomes a picture of the alienation of humanity from God.

8

JOSEPH, THE GOVERNOR

Joseph the dreamer had also from God the gift of interpreting dreams. Unjustly imprisoned in Egypt, he was able to interpret the dream of a fellow-prisoner, the king's steward. This steward was to remember Joseph when the king demanded an interpreter to show the meaning of two disturbing dreams, which had baffled the magicians and wise men of the land. In the first, seven fat cows had been feeding by the river when seven thin and bony cows came up out of the water and devoured them. In the second dream, seven thin ears of corn swallowed up seven full and ripe ones growing on the same stalk.

Because his gift of wisdom so impressed the king, Joseph finds himself in charge of nationwide arrangements against the coming famine. Under his protection and authority his whole extended family would leave their homeland, and settle as immigrants in Egypt.

Joseph said to the king, 'The two dreams mean the same thing; God has told you what he is going to do. The seven fat cows are seven years, and the seven full ears of corn are also seven years; they have the same meaning. The seven thin cows which came up later and the seven thin ears of corn scorched by the desert wind are seven years of famine. It is just as I told you — God has shown you what he is going to do. There will be seven years of great plenty in all the land of Egypt. After that, there will be seven years of famine, and all the good years will be forgotten, because the famine will ruin the country. The time of plenty will be entirely forgotten, because the famine which follows will be so terrible. The repetition of your dream means that the matter is fixed by God and that he will make it happen in the near future.

'Now you should choose some man with wisdom and insight and put him in charge of the country. You must also appoint other officials and take a fifth of the crops during the seven years of plenty. Order them to collect all the food during the good years that are coming, and give them authority to store up corn in the cities and guard it. The food will be a reserve supply for the country during the seven years of famine which are going to come on Egypt. In this way the people will not starve.'

The king and his officials approved this plan, and he said to them, 'We will never find a better man than Joseph, a man who has God's spirit in him.' The king said to Joseph, 'God has shown you all this, so it is obvious that you have greater wisdom and insight than anyone else. I will put you in charge of my country, and all my people will obey your orders. Your authority will be second only to mine. I now appoint you governor over all Egypt.' The king removed from his finger the ring engraved with the royal seal and put it on Joseph's finger. He put a fine linen robe on him, and placed a gold chain round his neck. He gave him the second royal chariot to ride in, and his guard of honour went ahead of him and cried out, 'Make way! Make way!' And so Joseph was appointed governor over all Egypt.

GENESIS 41:25-43 *GNB*

Jacob's family, driven by famine from their own country, prospered and multiplied in Egypt. But after Joseph's death the Egyptians began a systematic oppression of these Hebrew foreigners. The Hebrews became a race of slaves, toiling in the brick-fields and held in perpetual servitude.

Moreover, because their numbers increased, steps were taken to limit the growth of male population and so prevent any future uprising. The Egyptians planned to keep the Hebrews in their serfdom. But God had another purpose for his chosen people; and in Moses he gave them a leader who would set them on the road from Egyptian bondage to their own promised land.

A descendant of Levi married a Levite woman who conceived and bore a son. When she saw what a fine child he was, she hid him for three months, but she could conceal him no longer. So she got a rush basket for him, made it watertight with clay and tar, laid him in it, and put it among the reeds by the bank of the Nile. The child's sister took her stand at a distance to see what would happen to him. Pharaoh's daughter came down to bathe in the river, while her ladies-in-waiting walked along the bank. She noticed the basket among the reeds and sent her slave-girl for it. She took it from her and when she opened it, she saw the child. It was crying, and she was filled with pity for it. 'Why,' she said, 'it is a little Hebrew boy.' Thereupon the sister said to Pharaoh's daughter, 'Shall I go and fetch one of the Hebrew women as a wet-nurse to suckle the child for you?' Pharaoh's daughter told her to go; so the girl went and called the baby's mother. Then Pharaoh's daughter said to her, 'Here is the child, suckle him for me, and I will pay you for it myself.' So the woman took the child and suckled him. When the child was old enough, she brought him to Pharaoh's daughter, who adopted him and called him Moses, 'because', she said, 'I drew him out of the water.'

EXODUS 2:1-10 *NEB*

10

THE PASSOVER

Moses grew up to become the leader of his oppressed people in Egypt. Time and again on their behalf he asked the king of Egypt for permission to leave, but to no avail. God sent warnings and plagues (among them frogs, insects, boils, locusts, unnatural darkness) but still the king stubbornly refused.

So there came at last the final terrible judgment upon Egypt, the sentence of death on every eldest son. Moses and his people were to prepare themselves that same night to begin their journey to freedom, eating their 'Passover Festival' meal in haste, shod and dressed for travel. The lamb that was to be their supper was also to provide a sign to God's terrible angel to 'pass over' the Jewish households, and so save their first-born sons from death. The blood of the lamb was to be smeared on door-posts and lintels as God's saving token.

The Passover meal is still eaten in Jewish households to this day; for the Christian this ancient symbolism is perfectly fulfilled in Christ, the Lamb of God; whose blood, the apostle John tells us, 'cleanses us from all sin.'

Moses called for all the leaders of Israel and said to them, 'Each of you is to choose a lamb or a young goat and kill it, so that your families can celebrate Passover. Take a sprig of hyssop, dip it in the bowl containing the animal's blood, and wipe the blood on the door-posts and the beam above the door of your house. Not one of you is to leave the house until morning. When the Lord goes through Egypt to kill the Egyptians, he will see the blood on the beams and the door-posts and will not let the Angel of Death enter your houses and kill you. You and your children must obey these rules for ever. When you enter the land that the Lord has promised to give you, you must perform this ritual. When your children ask you, "What does this ritual mean?" you will answer, "It is the sacrifice of Passover to honour the Lord, because he passed over the houses of the Israelites in Egypt. He killed the Egyptians, but spared us."'

The Israelites knelt down and worshipped. Then they went and did what the Lord had commanded Moses and Aaron.

At midnight the Lord killed all the first-born sons in Egypt, from the king's son, who was heir to the throne, to the son of the prisoner in the dungeon; all the first-born of the animals were also killed. That night, the king, his officials, and all the other Egyptians were awakened. There was loud crying throughout Egypt, because there was not one home in which there was not a dead son. That same night the king sent for Moses and Aaron and said, 'Get out, you and your Israelites! Leave my country; go and worship the Lord, as you asked. Take your sheep, goats, and cattle, and leave. Also pray for a blessing on me.'

EXODUS 12:21-32 *GNB*

11

CROSSING THE RED SEA

Even after the many plagues, and the terrible experiences of Passover night, the king of Egypt was still unwilling to learn that no one can finally frustrate the purposes of God. John Stott writes: '"The Red Sea" which the escaping Israelites crossed was probably some shallow water north of the northern tip of the Suez Gulf. The miracle lay not in the "strong east wind" which parted the waters, but in the fact that God sent it at the very moment when "Moses stretched out his hand over the sea".' Just as Moses had been raised up at the Egyptian court in the providence of God to be the leader of his people, so God's care would continue to watch over them, and see his purpose and covenant fulfilled. Only their own disobedience would mar their destiny.

When the king of Egypt was told that the people had escaped, he and his officials changed their minds and said, 'What have we done? We have let the Israelites escape, and we have lost them as our slaves!' The king got his war chariot and his army ready. He set out with all his chariots, including the six hundred finest, commanded by their officers. The Lord made the king stubborn, and he pursued the Israelites, who were leaving triumphantly. The Egyptian army, with all the horses, chariots, and drivers, pursued them and caught up with them where they were camped by the Red Sea near Pi Hahiroth and Baal Zephon.

When the Israelites saw the king and his army marching against them, they were terrified and cried out to the Lord for help. They said to Moses, 'Weren't there any graves in Egypt? Did you have to bring us out here in the desert to die? Look what you have done by bringing us out of Egypt! Didn't we tell you before we left that this would happen? We told you to leave us alone and let us go on being slaves of the Egyptians. It would be better to be slaves there than to die here in the desert.'

Moses answered, 'Don't be afraid! Stand your ground, and you will see what the Lord will do to save you today; you will never see these Egyptians again. The Lord will fight for you, and there is no need for you to do anything.'

The Lord said to Moses, 'Why are you crying out for help? Tell the people to move forward. Lift up your stick and hold it out over the sea. The water will divide, and the Israelites will be able to walk through the sea on dry ground.'

Moses held out his hand over the sea, and the Lord drove the sea back with a strong east wind. It blew all night and turned the sea into dry land. The water was divided, and the Israelites went through the sea on dry ground, with walls of water on both sides.

EXODUS 14:5-16,21-22 *GNB*

MOSES, THE LAWGIVER

Moses led the people to Mount Sinai (probably in the South Sinai peninsula, where there are three contending locations). Here God undertook with Moses to 'come to you in a thick cloud, so that the people will hear me speaking with you'. When the day came, the mountain was enveloped in smoke and cloud; God called Moses to come alone to the mountain top, and there gave him the Law. It was to be part of God's covenant with his people that they should live in obedience to the Law that he gave them; and the 'ten commandments' as a framework for all ordered social life have stood the test of time. The first four speak of our duty to God — his exclusive worship, his holy name, his holy day of rest. The remainder concern our duty to our neighbour.

God spoke, and these were his words:

I am the Lord your God who brought you out of Egypt, out of the land of slavery.

You shall have no other god to set against me.

You shall not make a carved image for yourself nor the likeness of anything in the heavens above, or on the earth below, or in the waters under the earth.

You shall not bow down to them or worship them; for I, the Lord your God, am a jealous god. I punish the children for the sins of the fathers to the third and fourth generations of those who hate me. But I keep faith with thousands, with those who love me and keep my commandments.

You shall not make wrong use of the name of the Lord your God; the Lord will not leave unpunished the man who misuses his name.

Remember to keep the sabbath day holy. You have six days to labour and do all your work. But the seventh day is a sabbath of the Lord your God; that day you shall not do any work, you, your son or your daughter, your slave or your slave-girl, your cattle or the alien within your gates; for in six days the Lord made heaven and earth, the sea, and all that is in them, and on the seventh day he rested. Therefore the Lord blessed the sabbath day and declared it holy.

Honour your father and your mother, that you may live long in the land which the Lord your God is giving you.

You shall not commit murder.

You shall not commit adultery.

You shall not steal.

You shall not give false evidence against your neighbour.

You shall not covet your neighbour's house; you shall not covet your neighbour's wife, his slave, his slave-girl, his ox, his ass, or anything that belongs to him.

EXODUS 20:1-17 *NEB*

13

A SERPENT OF BRONZE

The people of Israel in their wilderness wanderings were given from God a covenant, a law and a pattern of religious ritual founded upon sacrifice. Yet their story is one of disobedience and rebellion which incurred the judgment of God. None of their adult generation, they were told, would enter the land of promise (with two faithful exceptions). They would spend forty years in the wilderness, as wandering nomads of the desert.

One of the punishments incurred during this time was a plague of poisonous snakes, deadly in their venom. The frightened tribesmen turned to Moses for help, who interceded with God for them. By this bronze serpent figure (still used today as a badge of healing) God showed mercy on his people, while driving home lessons of obedience and dependence.

Jesus was to use this story to point Nicodemus, one of the leading Pharisees of his day, to the meaning of faith. By it, he foreshadowed the cross on which he was to die; and introduced some of the most precious words in the New Testament: 'The Son of Man must be lifted above the heads of men — as Moses lifted up that serpent in the desert — so that any man who believes in him may have eternal life. For God loved the world so much that he gave his only Son so that everyone who believes in him should not be lost, but should have eternal life.' (John 3:15-16)

From Mount Hor they set out by the way to the Red Sea, to go around the land of Edom; and the people became impatient on the way. And the people spoke against God and against Moses, 'Why have you brought us up out of Egypt to die in the wilderness? For there is no food and no water, and we loathe this worthless food.' Then the Lord sent fiery serpents among the people, and they bit the people, so that many people of Israel died. And the people came to Moses, and said, 'We have sinned, for we have spoken against the Lord and against you; pray to the Lord, that he take away the serpents from us.' So Moses prayed for the people. And the Lord said to Moses, 'Make a fiery serpent, and set it on a pole; and every one who is bitten, when he sees it, shall live.' So Moses made a bronze serpent, and set it on a pole; and if a serpent bit any man, he would look at the bronze serpent and live.

NUMBERS 21:4-9 *RSV*

15

JOSHUA, THE NEW LEADER

In the early days of their wilderness wanderings, Moses had chosen Joshua as his assistant in the numerous military campaigns to which the people of Israel were committed. Joshua was one of only two men from among his generation who were to be allowed to enter the promised land, and on its borders he was formally appointed Moses' successor as leader of the people. To him was entrusted the crossing of the Jordan and the subduing of the Canaanites, a people whose religion 'appealed to the bestial and material in human nature'.

Joshua was neither simply chosen by Moses, nor elected by the people. His calling was from God himself, confirmed in this message of personal encouragement that God gave him at the start of his leadership. Because it speaks of God's faithfulness to his covenant promises, its meaning is not exhausted by the historical context in which these words were first given. Generations of God's servants, called to face new challenges, have turned to them for encouragement: 'As I was with Moses, so I will be with you . . . I will never forsake you.'

14

CHOOSE LIFE!

God had promised to Abraham a line of innumerable descendants, a world-wide family through whom God would work out his purposes for all humanity. God had also promised a land where his people might settle, and establish a community and nation faithful to himself. He had sent Moses to deliver them from Egyptian slavery and lead them to their promised land; but because of their disobedience they were unable to take possession of it for forty years.

As they stood on its borders, Moses reminded them of all that God had done for them. He himself belonged to the generation that would not possess the land. He therefore prepares to hand over the leadership to Joshua. Part of Moses' farewell message to those whom he had led and served was this call to renew their part of the covenant; to choose life, obedience, prosperity; and to confirm a relationship of love and worship with the Lord, the God of their ancestors and of themselves. The book of Deuteronomy ends with the Bible's divine tribute to Moses and his leadership. 'There has never been a prophet in Israel like Moses; the Lord spoke with him face to face. No other prophet has ever done miracles and wonders like those that the Lord sent Moses to perform...'

'Today I offer you the choice of life and good, or death and evil. If you obey the commandments of the Lord your God which I give you this day, by loving the Lord your God, by conforming to his ways and by keeping his commandments, statutes, and laws, then you will live and increase, and the Lord your God will bless you in the land which you are entering to occupy. But if your heart turns away and you do not listen and you are led on to bow down to other gods and worship them, I tell you this day that you will perish; you will not live long in the land which you will enter to occupy after crossing the Jordan. I summon heaven and earth to witness against you this day: I offer you the choice of life or death, blessing or curse. Choose life and then you and your descendants will live; love the Lord your God, obey him and hold fast to him: that is life for you and length of days in the land which the Lord swore to give to your forefathers, Abraham, Isaac and Jacob.'

DEUTERONOMY 30:15-20 *NEB*

After the death of Moses the servant of the Lord, the Lord said to Joshua son of Nun, Moses' assistant: 'Moses my servant is dead. Now then, you and all these people, get ready to cross the Jordan River into the land I am about to give to them — to the Israelites. I will give you every place where you set your foot, as I promised Moses. Your territory will extend from the desert to Lebanon, and from the great river, the Euphrates — all the Hittite country — to the Great Sea on the west. No-one will be able to stand up against you all the days of your life. As I was with Moses, so I will be with you; I will never leave you nor forsake you.

'Be strong and courageous, because you will lead these people to inherit the land I swore to their forefathers to give them. Be strong and very courageous. Be careful to obey all the law my servant Moses gave you: do not turn from it to the right or to the left, that you may be successful wherever you go. Do not let this Book of the Law depart from your mouth; meditate on it day and night, so that you may be careful to do everything written in it. Then you will be prosperous and successful. Have I not commanded you? Be strong and courageous. Do not be terrified; do not be discouraged, for the Lord your God will be with you wherever you go.'

JOSHUA 1:1-9 *NIV*

16

TAKING POSSESSION

Much of Old Testament history is a picture of God's faithfulness to an unfaithful people. By the end of Joshua's life, he was still reminding the people that they must keep their part of God's covenant. For the time there was peace; but the former inhabitants of the land, with their degraded morality and idolatrous worship were not finally driven out. Though the Lord had kept his promises, there was still to be a very unsettled period of Israel's history between the invasion of Canaan, and the setting up of an ordered kingdom. This was the period of the 'Judges' strong and individualistic leaders, operating a kind of martial law. The peace prevailing at the death of Joshua was to be short-lived indeed!

After a long time had passed and the Lord had given Israel rest from all their enemies around them, Joshua, by then old and well advanced in years, summoned all Israel — their elders, leaders, judges and officials — and said to them: 'I am old and well advanced in years. You yourselves have seen everything the Lord your God has done to all these nations for your sake; it was the Lord your God who fought for you . . .

'Now fear the Lord and serve him with all faithfulness. Throw away the gods your forefathers worshipped beyond the River and in Egypt, and serve the Lord. But if serving the Lord seems undesirable to you, then choose for yourselves this day whom you will serve, whether the gods your forefathers served beyond the River, or the gods of the Amorites, in whose land you are living. But as for me and my household, we will serve the Lord.'

JOSHUA 23:1-3; 24:14-15 *NIV*

17

THE CALL OF SAMUEL

During the period of the Judges, there was a priest called Eli responsible for the principal sanctuary of the Israelites at Shiloh. Here the early Tent of Meeting had long since given way to a more permanent sanctuary, the House of the Lord. Eli was old; and his two sons (who were also priests of this temple) were corrupt and worthless characters.

Samuel was dedicated to the Lord even before his birth. His mother Hannah had long been childless until in answer to her prayers God gave her Samuel. 'If you give me a son,' had been her prayer, 'I promise that I will dedicate him to you for his whole life.' As soon as he was old enough to be parted from her, his mother took him to Shiloh, to enter into the service of the temple. There, each year, she would come to visit him, taking 'a little robe' — each no doubt a size larger than the one before. It is quite a small child, therefore, whom God calls by name in the story that follows.

As the child grew, it was clear that the Lord was with him. It was said of him, 'When Samuel spoke, all Israel listened'. He was recognized as a prophet of the Lord; and it fell to him, in old age, to anoint Israel's first king.

Now the boy Samuel was ministering to the Lord under Eli. And the word of the Lord was rare in those days; there was no frequent vision. At that time Eli, whose eyesight had begun to grow dim, so that he could not see, was lying down in his own place; the lamp of God had not yet gone out, and Samuel was lying down within the temple of the Lord, where the ark of God was. Then the Lord called, 'Samuel! Samuel!' and he said, 'Here I am !' and ran to Eli, and said, 'Here I am, for you called me.' But he said, 'I did not call; lie down again.' So he went and lay down. And the Lord called again, 'Samuel!' And Samuel arose and went to Eli, and said, 'Here I am, for you called me.' But he said, 'I did not call, my son; lie down again.' Now Samuel did not yet know the Lord, and the word of the Lord had not yet been revealed to him. And the

Lord called Samuel again the third time. And he arose and went to Eli, and said, 'Here I am, for you called me.' Then Eli perceived that the Lord was calling the boy. Therefore Eli said to Samuel, 'Go, lie down; and if he calls you, you shall say, "Speak, Lord, for thy servant hears."'

So Samuel went and lay down in his place.

And the Lord came and stood forth, calling as at other times, 'Samuel! Samuel!' And Samuel said, 'Speak, for thy servant hears.'

I SAMUEL 3:1-10 *RSV*

18

THE SHEPHERD KING

The first book of Samuel is largely the story of Saul, who was anointed by Samuel to be the first king over Israel. Yet for his continued disobedience he was finally rejected, and the Bible pictures him as one of the most pathetic of all God's chosen servants.

Samuel is therefore commanded, as the Lord's prophet, to find and to anoint a new king in place of Saul — even though Saul still lived as king and clung to his throne. Samuel is told to seek out the family of Jesse 'for I have provided for myself a king among his sons'. He therefore summons and inspects each son in turn, without discerning in any of them a sign of the Lord's purpose. At last, in response to his enquiry, it transpires that Jesse has one more son, the youngest: and David is fetched from work. There and then, no doubt to the dismay of his elder brothers, David is anointed without further ceremony. A fine-looking country boy, he was not the tallest nor the strongest: but Samuel had been warned already that 'the Lord sees not as a man sees'.

None of those who witnessed this family drama would have foreseen that the boy king was also the forerunner of the Lord Jesus Christ, 'great David's greater Son'.

Samuel did what the Lord commanded, and came to Bethlehem. The elders of the city came to meet him trembling, and said, 'Do you come peaceably?' And he said, 'Peaceably; I have come to sacrifice to the Lord; consecrate yourselves, and come with me to the sacrifice.' And he consecrated Jesse and his sons, and invited them to the sacrifice.

When they came, he looked on Eliab and thought, 'Surely the Lord's anointed is before him.' But the Lord said to Samuel, 'Do not look on his appearance or on tthe height of his stature, because I have rejected him; for the Lord sees not as man sees; man looks on the outward appearance, but the Lord looks on the heart.' Then Jesse called Abinadab, and made him pass before Samuel. And he said, 'Neither has the Lord chosen this one.' Then Jesse made Shammah pass by. And he said, 'Neither has the Lord chosen this one.' And Jesse made seven of his sons pass before Samuel. And Samuel said to Jesse, 'The Lord has not chosen these.' And Samuel said to Jesse, 'Are all your sons here?' And he said, 'There remains yet the youngest, but behold, he is keeping the sheep.' And Samuel said to Jesse, 'Send and fetch him, for we will not sit down till he comes here.' And he sent, and brought him in. Now he was ruddy, and had beautiful eyes, and was handsome. And the Lord said, 'Arise, anoint him; for this is he.' Then Samuel took the horn of oil, and anointed him in the midst of his brothers; and the Spirit of the Lord came mightily upon David from that day forward. And Samuel rose up, and went to Ramah.

I SAMUEL 16:4-13 *RSV*

19

DAVID AND GOLIATH

In spite of David's anointing and his own rejection by God, Saul continued as king. David found a new role at court, ministering to Saul's fits of violence and depression (perhaps with some of the Psalms sung today in Christian worship) and becoming his armour-bearer.

David sprang to this new prominence by his single-handed defeat of the Philistine champion, the giant Goliath. Goliath challenged the Israelite army to produce a champion who would fight with him in single combat: 'If he wins, we will be your slaves; but if I win and kill him, you will be our slaves . . . I dare you to pick someone to fight me.' David, meanwhile, a shepherd-boy rather than a soldier, had been sent by his father to the front line to bring rations to his elder brothers. He heard the giant's boast, and offered to be the one to fight him — a laughable and ridiculous suggestion. Yet, for want of anyone better and persuaded by the boy's faith and courage, King Saul agreed. 'Go,' he said to him, 'and the Lord be with you.'

The rest is history. David achieved immense popularity with the people of Israel. Saul, fired by jealousy and fighting for his throne, pursued him relentlessly. Finally, when David was thirty, Saul was killed in battle and David's kingship was at last established.

Then David took his staff in his hand, and chose five smooth stones from the brook, and put them in his shepherd's bag, in his wallet; his sling was in his hand, and he drew near to the Philistine.

And the Philistine came on and drew near to David, with his shield-bearer in front of him. And when the Philistine looked, and saw David, he disdained him; for he was but a youth, ruddy and comely in appearance. And the Philistine said to David, 'Am I a dog, that you come to me with sticks?' And the Philistine cursed David by his gods. The Philistine said to David, 'Come to me, and I will give your flesh to the birds of the air and to the beasts of the field.' Then David said to the Philistine, 'You come to me with a sword and with a spear and with a javelin; but I come to you in the name of the Lord of hosts, the God of the armies of Israel, whom you have defied. This day the Lord will deliver you into my hand, and I will strike you down, and cut off your head; and I will give the dead bodies of the host of the Philistines this day to the birds of the air and the to the wild beasts of the earth; that all the earth may know that there is a God in Israel, and that all this assembly may know that the Lord saves not with sword and spear; for the battle is the Lord's and he will give you into our hand.'

When the Philistine arose and came and drew near to meet David, David ran quickly toward the battle line to meet the Philistine. And David put his hand in his bag and took out a stone, and slung it, and struck the Philistine on his forehead; the stone sank into his forehead, and he fell on his face to the ground.

So David prevailed over the Philistine with a sling and with a stone, and struck the Philistine, and killed him; there was no sword in the hand of David. Then David ran and stood over the Philistine, and took his sword and drew it out of its sheath, and killed him, and cut off his head with it. When the Philistines saw that their champion was dead, they fled.

I SAMUEL 17:40-51 *RSV*

20

KING SOLOMON

Solomon, famous alike for his wisdom and for his temple at Jerusalem, was David's son. It was understood that on his father's death he would succeed to the throne. When that time came, faced with his new responsibilities, God offered Solomon a choice of gifts, and commended him for asking for the gift of wisdom, an understanding heart.

His wisdom is illustrated in the celebrated dispute between two prostitutes who came to his court with a tiny baby. They lived together; each had a child; and in the night one of the two babies had died. Each claimed the surviving child as her own. Solomon's verdict was direct and simple. Cut the living child in two and give each woman half of it.' One of the two women agreed. The other pleaded for the life of the child, and was willing to surrender her claim rather than see it killed. It was not then difficult to determine who was the real mother! The story is told in I Kings 3:16-28.

Much of the Book of Proverbs is attributed to Solomon. His name is widely celebrated in the early folk-literature of the Middle East for his wisdom and for the splendour of his royal court. Jesus alluded to this legendary splendour when he called his hearers to look at the wild flowers on the hills about them, with the comment that 'even Solomon in all his glory was not arrayed like one of these'.

Now King Solomon went to Gibeon to offer a sacrifice, for that was the chief hill-shrine, and he used to offer a thousand whole-offerings on its altar. There that night the Lord God appeared to him in a dream and said, 'What shall I give you? Tell me.' And Solomon answered, 'Thou didst show great and constant love to thy servant David my father, because he walked before thee in loyalty, righteousness, and integrity of heart; and thou hast maintained this great and constant love towards him and hast now given him a son to succeed him on the throne. Now, O Lord my God, thou hast made thy servant king in place of my father David, though I am a mere child, unskilled in leadership. And I am here in the midst of thy people, the people of thy choice, too many to be numbered or counted. Give thy servant, therefore, a heart with skill to listen, so that he may govern thy people justly and distinguish good from evil. For who is equal to the task of governing this great people of thine?' The Lord was well pleased that Solomon had asked for this, and he said to him, 'Because you have asked for this, and not for long life for yourself, or for wealth, or for the lives of your enemies, but have asked for discernment in administering justice, I grant your request; I give you a heart so wise and so understanding that there has been none like you before your time nor will be after you. I give you furthermore those things for which you did not ask, such wealth and honour as no king of your time can match. And if you conform to my ways and observe my ordinances and commandments, as your father David did, I will give you long life.' Then he awoke, and knew it was a dream.

I KINGS 3:4-15 *NEB*

21

SOLOMON'S TEMPLE

The Book of Kings contains detailed descriptions of the magnificent Temple, the 'House of the Lord' which Solomon built on the east side of what is now the 'Old City' of Jerusalem. Sadly, for all his greatness, Solomon was not prepared to commit himself wholly to the Lord and to his covenant. His harem of foreign princesses 'turned his heart after other gods'.

Yet, like most of us, Solomon was a mixture. At the time when the Temple was completed, he showed in this great dedicatory prayer both his understanding of God's nature and covenant, and his own love and reverence for the Lord. The words reveal his exalted and spiritual view of deity — 'the heaven of heavens cannot contain thee' — and his recognition that kings and subjects alike stand in need of God's forgiveness and mercy. But, for all his wisdom, Solomon could not bring himself to be one of 'your servants who continue wholeheartedly in your way.' And of his great Temple, nothing now remains.

Then Solomon stood before the altar of the Lord in front of the whole assembly of Israel, spread out his hands towards heaven and said:

'O Lord, God of Israel, there is no God like you in heaven above or on earth below — you who keep your covenant of love with your servants who continue wholeheartedly in your way. You have kept your promise to your servant David my father; with your mouth you have promised and with your hand you have fulfilled it — as it is today.

'Now Lord, God of Israel, keep for your servant David my father the promises you made to him when you said, "You shall never fail to have a man to sit before me on the throne of Israel, if only your sons are careful in all they do to walk before me as you have done." And now, O God of Israel, let your word that you promised your servant David my father come true.

'But will God really dwell on earth? The heavens, even the highest heaven, cannot contain you. How much less this temple I have built! Yet give attention to your servant's prayer and his plea for mercy, O Lord my God. Hear the cry and the prayer that your servant is praying in your presence this day. May your eyes be open towards this temple night and day, this place of which you said, "My Name shall be there," so that you will hear the prayer your servant prays towards this place. Hear the supplication of your servant and of your people Israel when they pray towards this place. Hear from heaven, your dwelling-place, and when you hear, forgive.'

I KINGS 8:22-30 *NIV*

22

ELIJAH AND ELISHA

While David and Solomon reigned, their kingdom had been united. Now it divides into a northern kingdom of Israel and a southern kingdom of Judah. Still the story of God's unfaithful people continues; and a new prophet appears in the northern kingdom, the fiery Elijah. Together with Elisha his successor, he forms the link between the earlier prophets of Samuel's day, and the great prophets found in the second half of our Old Testament. At the heart of Elijah's ministry lies the continuing conflict between the worship of Baal, one of the heathen deities of the Canaanites, and the Lord, the true God of Israel.

Following the dramatic and spectacular overthrow of some of the prophets of Baal, when at Elijah's command fire fell from heaven upon the altar of the Lord, Elijah retreated in depression of spirit to a cave in the 'Mount of God' at Horeb. Horeb is the alternative name for Mount Sinai where God had revealed himself to Moses. Here God recommissions his disheartened servant, calling him to his final task and revealing to him the name of the prophet chosen to succeed him. Above all God shows him that he is not (as in his gloom he had begun to think) alone in his faithfulness; he is one of a great company of the Lord's people quite unknown to him, who share his resistance to Baal-worship.

Christians have always valued this revelation of God in the silence, the unspectacular, and the still small voice.

And there he came to a cave, and lodged there; and behold, the word of the Lord came to him, and he said to him, 'What are you doing here, Elijah?' He said, 'I have been very jealous for the Lord, the God of hosts; for the people of Israel have forsaken thy covenant, thrown down thy altars, and slain thy prophets with the sword; and I, even I only, am left; and they seek my life, to take it away.' And he said, 'Go forth, and stand upon the mount before the Lord.' And behold, the Lord passed by, and a great and strong wind rent the mountains, and broke in pieces the rocks before the Lord, but the Lord was not in the wind; and after the wind an earthquake, but the Lord was not in the earthquake; and after the earthquake a fire, but the Lord was not in the fire; and after the fire a still small voice. And when Elijah heard it, he wrapped his face in his mantle and went out and stood at the entrance of the cave. And behold, there came a voice to him, and said,

'What are you doing here, Elijah?' He said, 'I have been very jealous for the Lord, the God of hosts; for the people of Israel have forsaken thy covenant, thrown down thy altars, and slain thy prophets with the sword; and I, even I only, am left; and they seek my life, to take it away.' And the Lord said to him, 'Go, return on your way to the wilderness of Damascus; and when you arrive, you shall anoint Hazael to be king over Syria; and Jehu the son of Nimshi you shall anoint to be king over Israel; and Elisha the son of Shaphat of Abel-meholah you shall anoint to be prophet in your place. And him who escapes from the sword of Hazael shall Jehu slay; and him who escapes from the sword of Jehu shall Elisha slay. Yet I will leave seven thousand in Israel, all the knees that have not bowed to Baal, and every mouth that has not kissed him.'

I KINGS 19:9-18 *RSV*

23

ELISHA AND NAAMAN

The prophet Elisha, Elijah's chosen successor, shared with him a God-given ability to work miracles. This story of the healing of the Commander-in-Chief of the Aramaean army is a celebrated account of the exercise of his powers in response to faith. The story begins with the word of a servant girl. Then there follows the journey to Israel, a foreign and generally hostile power, only to be met with a humiliating message from the prophet who did not even appear in person to greet him. It is not surprising that Naaman 'went away in a rage'. He had a clear mental picture of how a prophet should behave to a distinguished visitor and what he should do to work the miracle. His mind was closed to anything else.

Preachers have seen in this story a parable of the gospel. Naaman's leprosy here stands for an image of human sinfulness and need. It afflicts small and great alike; it is no respecter of persons. Good news of deliverance comes to us from unlikely sources; and requires an act of faith. God's way of salvation through the cross of Christ is not at all what we expect. For many people it appears too humbling and simplistic; we have our own very different ideas of how we would like our problems to be met. But God has chosen for his purposes the obedience of faith; and the principles that were at work in the healing of Naaman are a vivid illustration of God's offer of salvation to those prepared to take him at his word.

Naaman came with his horses and chariots and stood at the entrance to Elisha's house. Elisha sent out a messenger to say to him, 'If you will go and wash seven times in the Jordan, your flesh will be restored and you will be clean.' Naaman was furious and went away, saying, 'I thought he would at least have come out and stood, and invoked the Lord his God by name, waved his hand over the place and so rid me of the disease. Are not Abana and Pharpar, rivers of Damascus, better than all the waters of Israel? Can I not wash in them and be

THE WATERS OF BABYLON

clean?' So he turned and went off in a rage. But his servants came up to him and said, 'If the prophet had bidden you do something difficult, would you not do it? How much more then, if he tells you to wash and be clean?' So he went down and dipped himself in the Jordan seven times as the man of God had told him, and his flesh was restored as a little child's, and he was clean.

2 KINGS 5:9-14 *NEB*

In the perspective of history, the divided kingdom did not last long. Two centuries after the death of Solomon Samaria fell to the Assyrians, and the northern kingdom of Israel passed into captivity. After two more centuries Jerusalem fell to the Babylonians, the people of Judah were deported into exile, the city sacked and the temple destroyed. This exile is depicted by the prophets as the judgment of God upon a people who were consistently faithless and disobedient — but whom he still loved and yearned for. Still his patience was not exhausted; and by the end of the century the exiles were returning and the temple re-opened. This short psalm speaks eloquently of the pains of exile. 'Zion' is one of the names given to the city of Jerusalem.

The temple in Jerusalem continued to have a stormy history. The later building which Jesus knew (called by historians 'Herod's Temple') was only completed in AD64; though the main structure had been finished a few years before Jesus was born. In AD70 it was finally destroyed at the hands of the occupying Romans.

By the rivers of Babylon we sat and wept
    when we remembered Zion.
There on the poplars
    we hung our harps,
for there our captors asked us for songs,
    our tormentors demanded songs of joy;
they said, 'Sing us one of the songs of Zion!'

How can we sing the songs of the Lord
    while in a foreign land?
If I forget you, O Jerusalem,
    may my right hand forget its skill.
May my tongue cling to the roof of my mouth
    if I do not remember you,
if I do not consider Jerusalem
    my highest joy.

PSALM 137:1-6 *NIV*

The Book of Job explores the problem of human suffering. The story opens with Job, wealthy and God-fearing. The writer of the book pictures a dialogue between God and Satan, in which God commends Job's faithfulness, and Satan is scornful of it. 'Let him taste suffering,' says Satan, 'and he will curse you to your face.' God takes up the challenge and gives permission.

The greater part of the book goes on to describe Job wrestling to understand his new and terrible predicament. His wealth is gone, his family killed, his body covered with boils and sores. One by one, his friends come to talk with him (Job's comforters, we call them) but to no avail. Finally God's own voice is heard, reducing Job to silence as he compares the littleness of man, the creature, with the greatness of God the Creator. Job humbles himself. Though questions remain unanswered, he has caught a vision of God, and his faith is renewed: 'I see thee with my own eyes . . . I repent in dust and ashes.' He surrenders himself and his suffering into the hands of God.

In wonderful poetic language God begins by describing to Job the unimaginable: the creation of earth; the placing of stars; form and colour, sea and cloud, life and death.

Then the Lord answered Job out of the tempest:

Who is this whose ignorant words
cloud my design in darkness?
Brace yourself and stand up like a man;
I will ask questions, and you shall answer.
Where were you when I laid the earth's
    foundations?
Tell me, if you know and understand.
Who settled its dimensions? Surely you should
    know.
Who stretched his measuring-line over it?
On what do its supporting pillars rest?
Who set its corner-stone in place,
when the morning stars sang together
and all the sons of God shouted aloud?
Who watched over the birth of the sea,
when it burst in flood from the womb? —
when I wrapped it in a blanket of cloud
and cradled it in fog,
when I established its bounds,
fixing its doors and bars in place,
and said, 'Thus far shall you come and no
    farther,

and here your surging waves shall halt.'
In all your life have you ever called up the dawn
or shown the morning its place?
Have you taught it to grasp the fringes of
    the earth
and shake the Dog-star from its place;
to bring up the horizon in relief as clay under
    a seal,
until all things stand out like the folds of a
    cloak,
when the light of the Dog-star is dimmed
and the stars of the Navigator's Line go out
    one by one?
Have you descended to the springs of the sea
or walked in the unfathomable deep?
Have the gates of death been revealed to you?
Have you ever seen the door-keepers of the place
    of darkness?
Have you comprehended the vast expanse of
    the world?
Come, tell me all this, if you know.

JOB 38:1-18 *NEB*

26

THE SHEPHERD PSALM

When we were first introduced to David he was 'keeping the sheep'. Later, at court, he sang and played to King Saul, soothing and calming his moods of depression and violence. So this best-loved of all the psalms comes directly from his experience, and may have spoken to the heart of Saul, just as it has spoken to millions down the centuries, of God's shepherding care.

Not surprisingly, in its simplicity and strength, it is a part of the Bible which proves particularly precious in the face of death. The valley of the shadow is real enough; but not more so than the presence of the Lord and the promise of his eternal home.

The Lord is my shepherd; I shall not want.
He maketh me to lie down in green pastures:
he leadeth me beside the still waters.
He restoreth my soul: he leadeth me in the paths of righteousness for his name's sake.
Yea, though I walk through the valley of the shadow of death,
I will fear no evil: for thou art with me; thy rod and thy staff they comfort me.
Thou preparest a table before me in the presence of mine enemies:
thou anointest my head with oil; my cup runneth over.
Surely goodness and mercy shall follow me all the days of my life:
and I will dwell in the house of the Lord for ever.

PSALM 23 *KJV*

27

FAR ABOVE RUBIES

The Book of Proverbs, long associated with King Solomon and his gift of wisdom, begins with words that explain its purpose: 'That men may know wisdom and instruction, understand words of insight, receive instruction in wise dealing, righteousness, justice, and equity; that prudence may be given to the simple, knowledge and discretion to the youth . . . '

Much of the book consists of short pithy sayings, the fruit of long experience in that art of living which takes account of the purposes of God. This final chapter is a celebrated description of a virtuous woman, who has built her life upon just the sort of divine wisdom that the book is written to impart. The King James translation describes such a wife as precious 'far above rubies'.

A good wife who can find?
   She is far more precious than jewels.
The heart of her husband trusts in her,
   and he will have no lack of gain.
She does him good, and not harm,
   all the days of her life.
She seeks wool and flax,
   and works with willing hands.
She is like the ships of the merchant,
   she brings her food from afar.
She rises while it is yet night
   and provides food for her household
   and tasks for her maidens.
She considers a field and buys it;
   with the fruit of her hands she plants a vineyard.
She girds her loins with strength and makes her arms strong.
She perceives that her merchandise is profitable.
   Her lamp does not go out at night.
She puts her hands to the distaff,
   and her hands hold the spindle.
She opens her hands to the poor,
   and reaches out her hands to the needy.
She is not afraid of snow for her household,
   for all her household are clothed in scarlet.
She makes herself coverings;
   her clothing is fine linen and purple.
Her husband is known in the gates,
   when he sits among the elders of the land.
She makes linen garments and sells them;
   she delivers girdles to the merchant.
Strength and dignity are her clothing,
   and she laughs at the time to come.
She opens her mouth with wisdom,
   and the teaching of kindness is on her tongue.
She looks well to the ways of her household,
   and does not eat the bread of idleness.
Her children rise up and call her blessed;
   her husband also, and he praises her:
'Many women have done excellently,
   but you surpass them all.'
Charm is deceitful, and beauty is vain,
   but a woman who fears the Lord is to be praised.

PROVERBS 31:10-30 *RSV*

28

ALL IN VAIN?

OLD TESTAMENT

This famous exhortation, with its vivid description of old age, concludes the book of Ecclesiastes — a study of the emptiness of a life which has found no spiritual dimension or eternal perspective, where all is finally in vain.

But there are glimpses of something better: of an eternal home, of a spirit returning to God who made it.

The key to much of the imagery is to see in this passage a picture of old age. Look for the trembling hands (the 'keepers of the house'),

the bent knees, the teeth fewer and the eyes dim. Confidence is shaken, the hair whitens like almond-blossom, desire fails. Finally the potter's work is broken, the cord of life severed, flesh and spirit part. And was it all 'vanity' — that is, all in vain? The last verse of the book tells us otherwise. It points us beyond ourselves to God — to that Creator who beckons us 'in the days of our youth' and through the whole of life as the One who alone can give it meaning.

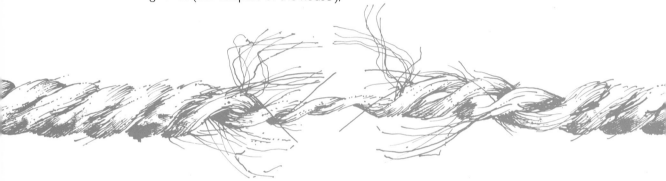

Remember also your Creator in the days of your youth, before the evil days come, and the years draw nigh, when you will say, 'I have no pleasure in them'; before the sun and the light, and the moon, and the stars are darkened and the clouds return after the rain; in the day when the keepers of the house tremble, and the strong men are bent, and the grinders cease because they are few, and those that look through the window are dimmed, and the doors on the street are shut; when the sound of the grinding is low, and one rises up at the voice of a bird, and all the daughters of song are brought low; they are afraid also of what is high, and terrors are in the way; the almond tree blossoms, the grasshopper drags itself along and desire fails; because man goes to his eternal home, and the mourners go about the streets; before the silver cord is snapped, or the golden bowl is broken, or the pitcher is broken at the fountain, or the wheel broken at the cistern, and the dust returns to the earth as it was, and the spirit returns to God who gave it. Vanity of vanities, says the Preacher; all is vanity. . .

The end of the matter; all has been heard. Fear God, and keep his commandments; for this is the whole duty of man. For God will bring every deed into judgment, with every secret thing, whether good or evil.

ECCLESIASTES 12:1-8,13-14 *RSV*

29

THE VISION OF GOD

Much of the earlier part of the Old Testament is in the form of history; while from this point onwards we are reading prophecy. The word does not mean (as we tend to think, when we use it in ordinary speech) the foretelling of the future, though it may include that. Rather, a prophet is someone to whom God reveals himself, his purposes, and his word for that generation. He becomes the person through whom God speaks.

This short passage is an account of the calling of Isaiah to be just such a messenger. Isaiah is one of the very greatest of the Old Testament prophets. There is a tradition that he was of royal blood and therefore familiar with earthly courts and kings. So for all its apparent simplicity, Isaiah's vision is profound. The Lord is reigning as a great king (the throne), over all things (high and exalted), divine (in a temple). Heavenly messengers obey him, holiness characterizes him, and though he is in heaven, his glory fills our earth. As on Sinai when God appeared to Moses, his presence is felt in smoke and earthquake. Above all, Isaiah's vision gave him a new glimpse, not only of God but of himself. Before the Lord could call or use him, his sinfulness must be dealt with in the purifying fire of God.

In the year that King Uzziah died, I saw the Lord seated on a throne, high and exalted, and the train of his robe filled the temple. Above him were seraphs, each with six wings: With two wings they covered their faces, with two they covered their feet, and with two they were flying. And they were calling to one another:

'Holy, holy, holy is the Lord God Almighty: the whole earth is full of his glory.'

At the sound of their voices the doorposts and thresholds shook and the temple was filled with smoke.

'Woe to me!' I cried. 'I am ruined! For I am a man of unclean lips, and I live among a people of unclean lips, and my eyes have seen the King, the Lord Almighty.'

Then one of the seraphs flew to me with a live coal in his hand, which he had taken with tongs from the altar. With it he touched my mouth and said, 'See, this has touched your lips; your guilt is taken away and your sin atoned for.'

Then I heard the voice of the Lord saying, 'Whom shall I send? And who will go for us?'

And I said, 'Here am I. Send me!'

ISAIAH 6:1-8 *NIV*

30

A MAN OF SORROWS

A vision of the future is only a part of prophecy. Yet it is impossible to read this moving account of God's suffering servant in the book of Isaiah without seeing clearly depicted the sufferings of Jesus centuries later.

These verses are poetry, part of what are called 'the Servant Songs'. It is not possible to say with certainty to whom they referred in the prophet's mind. Was it to a future Messiah; or to the nation of Israel, the Lord's people undergoing suffering and oppression; or to the prophet himself, unpopular because of his faithfulness to God's call; or to some other king or prophet or national figure? But the Lord's prophets usually speak more than even they themselves can fully understand and contemporary interpretations do not exhaust their inspired messages. Jesus applied a later section of this prophecy to himself and his mission on his way to the Garden of Gethsemane in his final hour of freedom.

Who has believed what we have heard?
 And to whom has the arm of the Lord been revealed?
For he grew up before him like a young plant,
 and like a root out of dry ground;
he had no form or comeliness that we should look at him,
 and no beauty that we should desire him.
He was despised and rejected by men;
 a man of sorrows, and acquainted with grief;
and as one from whom men hide their faces
 he was despised, and we esteemed him not.

Surely he has borne our griefs
 and carried our sorrows;
yet we esteemed him stricken,
 smitten by God, and afflicted.
But he was wounded for our transgressions,
 he was bruised for our iniquities;
upon him was the chastisement that made us whole,
 and with his stripes we are healed.
All we like sheep have gone astray;
 we have turned every one to his own way;
and the Lord has laid on him
 the iniquity of us all.

ISAIAH 53:1-6 *RSV*

THE POTTER'S HOUSE

About a hundred years separate Jeremiah from Isaiah. He was still young when the Lord called him to be a prophet. His task was to preach repentance to a people unwilling to listen. His love went out to them (as a true prophet's must) even in their waywardness. They hated him and persecuted him in return. More than once the prophecy that he was given came to him in symbol as well as word; and here we have a vivid picture of God the Creator shaping the nation, as a potter forms the soft clay spinning on his wheel. Let the clay prove stubborn, the shape miscarry — and the whole pot reverts at once to a formless lump of clay, from which quite another pot must now be formed.

Faced with this dramatic presentation, a memorable and vivid oracle of judgment, the people of Jerusalem hardened their hearts against both the prophet and the Lord who had called him. God had warned him that his fellow-citizens would not listen; and no more they did. His greatness lies in his faithfulness to God's call, and in his clear vision of true religion as a matter of the heart. He affirmed that in the exile that awaited them,

the Jewish nation — even deprived of homeland, priests and temple — could still worship the living God who shapes our destinies in love, as the potter shapes the clay.

This is the word that came to Jeremiah from the Lord, 'Go down to the potter's house, and there I will give you my message.' So I went down to the potter's house, and I saw him working at the wheel. But the pot he was shaping from the clay was marred in his hands; so the potter formed it into another pot, shaping it as seemed best to him.

Then the word of the Lord came to me: 'O house of Israel, can I not do with you as this potter does?' declares the Lord. 'Like clay in the hand of the potter, so are you in my hand, O house of Israel. If at any time I announce that a nation or kingdom is to be uprooted, torn down and destroyed, and if that nation I warned repents of its evil, then I will relent and not inflict on it the disaster I had planned. And if at another time I announce that a nation or kingdom is to be built up and planted, and if it does evil in my sight and does not obey me, then I will reconsider the good I had intended to do for it.

'Now therefore say to the people of Judah and those living in Jerusalem, "This is what the Lord says: Look! I am preparing a disaster for you and devising a plan against you. So turn from your evil ways, each one of you, and reform your ways and your actions." But they will reply, "It's no use. We will continue with our own plans; each of us will follow the stubbornness of his evil heart."'

JEREMIAH 18:1-12 *NIV*

32

THE VALLEY OF DRY BONES

Isaiah, Jeremiah and Ezekiel form a trio of major prophets; between them they account for two-thirds of all Old Testament prophecy. Ezekiel brought the word of the Lord to a shaken and demoralized people in exile. In a series of visions he makes it clear that God's omnipotence cannot be limited by the failure of his people. Perhaps the most powerful and vivid of them is this wonderful description of how under the influence of the word and the Spirit of God, dry dismembered bones can be re-clothed with life and power.

This is a promise to Israel of more than restoration. The picture is of a new creation; a repetition of the scene when God, in the beginning, formed Adam from the dust of the ground 'and breathed into his nostrils the breath of life; and man became a living being'. This same principle of God as the one who brings life out of death runs all through Scripture, finding a fulfilment in the resurrection of Jesus Christ, and the new life breathed upon the infant church on the day of Pentecost.

And what Ezekiel saw in this vision symbolizes a fact of present experience. Many would testify that their lives were like this valley of bones 'dried up, without any hope and with no future'. Yet by his word and Spirit, through faith in Christ, there comes a re-birth to life, purpose, meaning and power.

I felt the powerful presence of the Lord, and his spirit took me and set me down in a valley where the ground was covered with bones. He led me all round the valley, and I could see that there were very many bones and that they were very dry. He said to me, 'Mortal man, can these bones come back to life?'

I replied, 'Sovereign Lord, only you can answer that!'

He said, 'Prophesy to the bones. Tell these dry bones to listen to the word of the Lord. Tell them that I, the Sovereign Lord, am saying to them: I am going to put breath into you and bring you back to life. I will give you sinews and muscles, and cover you with skin. I will put breath into you and bring you back to life. Then you will know that I am the Lord.'

So I prophesied as I had been told. While I was speaking, I heard a rattling noise, and the bones began to join together. While I watched, the bones were covered with sinews and muscles, and then with skin. But there was no breath in the bodies.

God said to me, 'Mortal man, prophesy to the wind. Tell the wind that the Sovereign Lord commands it to come from every direction, to breathe into these dead bodies, and to bring them back to life.'

So I prophesied as I had been told. Breath entered the bodies, and they came to life and stood up. There were enough of them to form an army.

God said to me, 'Mortal man, the people of Israel are like these bones. They say that they are dried up, without any hope and with no future. So prophesy to my people Israel and tell them that I, the Sovereign Lord, am going to open their graves. I am going to take them out and bring them back to the land of Israel. When I open the graves where my people are buried and bring them out, they will know that I am the Lord. I will put my breath in them, bring them back to life, and let them live in their own land. Then they will know that I am the Lord. I have promised that I would do this — and I will. I, the Lord, have spoken.'

EZEKIEL 37:1-14 *GNB*

33

DANIEL

Daniel was an Israelite, perhaps the son of a noble family, carried into exile in Babylon. Like Joseph of old, he impressed his captors with his wisdom and usefulness. He rose to hold high office; promoted perhaps over the heads of local officers, who schemed to bring about his downfall. Daniel's position seemed however to be impregnable, his reputation unassailable. They agreed, 'We shall not find any ground or complaint against this Daniel unless we find it in connection with the law of his God.'

So, with great cunning, they persuaded the king to sign a decree, unalterable and final, that it should be forbidden for thirty days to make any petition, whether to God or man, except to the king himself; and that any offender should be thrown to the lions. They had reckoned, rightly, that Daniel was not one to yield to threats, or to obey earthly rulers rather than God.

When Daniel heard that the document had been signed, he retired to his house. The windows of his upstairs room faced towards Jerusalem. Three times each day he continued to fall on his knees, praying and giving praise to God as he had always done. These men came along in a body and found Daniel praying and pleading with God. They then came to the king and said, 'Have you not just signed an edict forbidding any man for the next thirty days to pray to anyone, god or man, other than to yourself O king, on pain of being thrown into the lions' den?' 'The decision stands,' the king replied 'as befits the law of the Medes and the Persians, which cannot be revoked.' Then they said to the king, 'O king, this man Daniel, one of the exiles from Judah, disregards both you and the edict which you have signed: he is at his prayers three times each day.' When the king heard these words he was deeply distressed, and determined to save Daniel; he racked his brains until sunset to find some way out. But the men came back in a body to the king and said, 'O king, remember that in conformity with the law of the Medes and Persians, no edict or decree can be altered when once issued by the king.'

The king then ordered Daniel to be fetched and thrown into the lion pit. The king said to Daniel, 'Your God himself, whom you have served so faithfully, will have to save you.' A stone was then brought and laid over the mouth of the pit; and the king sealed it with his own signet and with that of his noblemen, so that there could be no going back on the original decision about Daniel. The king returned to his palace, spent the night in fasting and refused to receive any of his concubines. Sleep eluded him, and at the first sign of dawn he was up, and hurried off to the lion pit. As he approached the pit he shouted in anguished tones, 'Daniel, servant of the living God! Has your God, whom you serve so faithfully, been able to save you from the lions?' Daniel replied, 'O king, live for ever! My God sent his angel who sealed the lions' jaws, they did me no harm, since in his sight I am blameless, and I have never done you any wrong either, O king.' The king was overjoyed, and ordered Daniel to be released from the pit. Daniel was released from the pit, and found to be quite unhurt, because he had trusted in his God.

DANIEL 6:10-24 JB

34

JUSTICE AND RIGHTEOUSNESS

The Old Testament ends with twelve short books, the 'Minor Prophets'. In the Hebrew Bible they are not twelve books but one; and the word 'minor' (which was attached to them comparatively late in the day) refers to their length, not their significance. In their short books they contain some of the clearest teaching about God's love and righteousness, his concern for the poorest of his people, his desire for a worship that is of the heart.

Amos, in common with other prophets of the Lord, is called to pronounce God's displeasure with his people Israel. They are offending against the moral law of God. They claim to look forward to the 'Day of the Lord', when God would appear to vindicate his people and scatter their enemies. Amos tells them that it will not be like that at all. All their worship is vain and empty while there is no justice nor righteousness in their dealings with one another; and especially with the poor, the helpless and the weak. In language that his hearers must have found almost unbelievable, Amos preached the worthlessness of religious observance divorced from obedience and social righteousness. Before our worship can be acceptable to God, our hearts must submit to his demands in obedience to the laws he gives us for our life together.

Woe to you who long for the day of the Lord!
　Why do you long for the day of the Lord?
　That day will be darkness, not light.
It will be as though a man fled from a lion
　only to meet a bear,
as though he entered his house
　and rested his hand on the wall
　only to have a snake bite him . . .

I hate, I despise your religious feasts;
　I cannot stand your assemblies.
Even though you bring me burnt offerings and
　　　grain offerings,
　I will not accept them.
Though you bring choice fellowship offerings,
　I will have no regard for them.
Away with the noise of your songs!
　I will not listen to the music of your harps.
But let justice roll on like a river,
　righteousness like a never-failing stream!

AMOS 5:18-19,21-24 *NIV*

35

WHAT DOES GOD ASK?

Like almost all the Old Testament prophets, Micah's message must have made painful hearing. Israel thought of herself as the Lord's chosen people — and was right to do so. Precisely because of this, prophet after prophet was called to denounce her sins, oppressions and injustices. And when, as so often, these were accompanied by a proud show of religion, they met the fiercer condemnation.

In this famous passage, Micah reminds his hearers of that inner light and voice of conscience, instructed over many centuries, but to which they would not listen. Without 'clean hands and a pure heart' there could be no possible way into the presence of a holy God — not with thousands of burnt-offerings or rivers of precious oil (fruit of the olive, part of the offerings of the temple worship) nor even with the perverted excesses of human sacrifice, as in idolatrous and heathen worship.

And yet the best of Micah's hearers knew that, modest as the Lord's requirements seem, they were beyond human reach. All the long history of Israel went to prove that unaided and unredeemed the heart of man cannot settle for long to justice and mercy and a humble obedience of love. The Old Testament has had signs and shadows of God's answer to the problem of human waywardness and self-centredness. In the New Testament, it becomes the dominant and triumphant theme.

How shall I come into the presence of the Lord,
And bow myself low before the most high God?
Shall I approach him with burnt-offerings —
   with calves a full year old?
Will the Lord be pleased with thousands of rams,
With ten thousand rivers of oil?
Shall I give my first-born to pay for my own misdeeds —
The fruit of my flesh for the sin of my soul?

You know well enough, Man, what is good!
For what does the Lord require from you,
But to be just, to love mercy,
And to walk humbly with your God?

MICAH 6:6-8 *JBP*

36

THE WORD MADE FLESH

The story of Jesus in the four Gospels often appears the most straightforward part of the Bible, the portrait of an individual conveyed in stories of his life and teaching. But this first chapter of John is not at all like that.

John was writing for those brought up in the Greek culture of much of the civilized world about him. He begins therefore with 'the Word', our translation for what the Greeks thought of as the creative and life-giving principle behind the universe. Greek philosophy held it to be the instrument through which our world was called into being and held together, 'the thought of God stamped upon the universe'.

So John begins with the astonishing statement that this divine principle has become a man — been 'made flesh' — and entered our world as one of us. That same Jesus of Nazareth, whose story John is about to tell, is God's Word to us. He comes to bring light and life to the dark places of our lives, even as God's creative word brought light and order into primeval darkness and chaos at the formation of the world.

In the beginning was the Word, and the Word was with God, and the Word was God. He was in the beginning with God; all things were made through him, and without him was not anything made that was made. In him was life, and the life was the light of men. The light shines in the darkness, and the darkness has not overcome it . . .

The true light that enlightens every man was coming into the world. He was in the world, and the world was made through him, yet the world knew him not. He came to his own home, and his own people received him not. But to all who received him, who believed in his name, he gave power to become children of God; who were born, not of blood nor of the will of the flesh nor of the will of man, but of God.

And the Word became flesh and dwelt among us, full of grace and truth; we have beheld his glory, glory as of the only Son from the Father.

JOHN 1:1-5,9-14 *RSV*

THE LORD'S SERVANT

God has a way of choosing unlikely means to bring about his purposes. When the moment came for God himself, in the person of his Son, to enter the world as one of us, he chose to do so by human birth. So he sends word by the angel Gabriel (who stands in the presence of God) to Mary, a village girl of Nazareth. She is soon to be married to Joseph, the local carpenter or builder. Gabriel tells her of the son she is to bear in whom the promises of the ages would be fulfilled — promises to David and to Jacob, centuries before. God's Son would have in Mary a human mother; and her husband would be to him in every way a human father — in every way, that is, but one. For this child is to be of divine, not human paternity. As the ancient creeds of the church say, he would be 'conceived by the Holy Spirit, born of the Virgin Mary'.

And to all this, at whatever cost to her own hopes, her reputation in the village, her privacy and peace of heart, Mary gives willing obedience. Her trust is in God, and she knows his plans are best.

In the sixth month, God sent the angel Gabriel to Nazareth, a town in Galilee, to a virgin pledged to be married to a man named Joseph, a descendant of David. The virgin's name was Mary. The angel went to her and said, 'Greetings, you who are highly favoured! The Lord is with you.'

Mary was greatly troubled at his words and wondered what kind of greeting this might be. But the angel said to her, 'Do not be afraid, Mary, you have found favour with God. You will be with child and give birth to a son, and you are to give him the name Jesus. He will be great and will be called the Son of the Most High. The Lord God will give him the throne of his father David, and he will reign over the house of Jacob for ever; his kingdom will never end.'

'How will this be,' Mary asked the angel, 'since I am a virgin?'

The angel answered, 'The Holy Spirit will come upon you, and the power of the Most High will overshadow you. So the holy one to be born will be called the Son of God.' . . .

'I am the Lord's servant,' Mary answered. 'May it be to me as you have said.' Then the angel left her.

LUKE 1:26-35,38 *NIV*

THE BIRTH OF JESUS CHRIST

John wrote that 'the Word became flesh'. Here Luke (an accurate and careful historian) describes the night on which that divine 'Word' came into the world. Legends and fairy stories like to begin 'Long, long ago . . .', 'Once upon a time . . .' Note the difference in this account. Caesar Augustus and Quirinius are readily identifiable in Roman history. Syria, Judaea, Galilee, Nazareth, Bethlehem are real places on the world's map.

Mary had been told that the holy child she was to bear would be called the Son of the Most High. Now the shepherds hear that he is both a saviour and also 'Christ the Lord', the promised Messiah (which means 'the Anointed One'). For centuries the Jews had been awaiting the coming of the Messiah. He was to be the one through whom their destiny, within their long covenant-relationship with God, would be finally fulfilled.

'Christ' is the Greek translation of 'Messiah'. Jesus Christ is not therefore a family name like John Smith, a given name coupled with a family name. It means 'Jesus the Messiah' or 'Jesus, the Anointed One of God'.

Now at this time Caesar Augustus issued a decree for a census of the whole world to be taken. This census — the first — took place while Quirinius was governor of Syria, and everyone went to his own town to be registered. So Joseph set out from the town of Nazareth in Galilee and travelled up to Judaea, to the town of David called Bethlehem, since he was of David's House and line, in order to be registered together with Mary, his betrothed, who was with child. While they were there the time came for her to have her child, and she gave birth to a son, her first-born. She wrapped him in swaddling clothes, and laid him in a manger because there was no room for them at the inn. In the countryside close by there were shepherds who lived in the fields and took it in turns to watch their flocks during the night. The angel of the Lord appeared to them and the glory of the Lord shone round them. They were terrified, but the angel said, 'Do not be afraid. Listen, I bring you news of great joy, a joy to be shared by the whole people. Today in the town of David a saviour has been born to you; he is Christ the

Lord. And here is a sign for you; you will find
a baby wrapped in swaddling clothes and lying
in a manger.' And suddenly with the angel there
was a great throng of the heavenly host, praising
God and singing:

> 'Glory to God in the highest heaven,
> and peace to men who enjoy his favour.'

Now when the angels had gone from them into
heaven, the shepherds said to one another, 'Let
us go to Bethlehem and see this thing that has
happened which the Lord has made known to
us'. So they hurried away and found Mary and
Joseph, and the baby lying in the manger. When
they saw the child they repeated what they had
been told about him, and everyone who heard
it was astonished at what the shepherds had
to say. As for Mary, she treasured all these
things and pondered them in her heart. And
the shepherds went back glorifying and praising
God for all they had heard and seen; it was
exactly as they had been told.

LUKE 2:1-20 *JB*

39

WISE MEN FROM THE EAST

Angels, shepherds and wise men are the familiar characters of the Christmas story. They feature on our cards and in our carols. These wise men (sometimes called Magi, related to the word 'magician') were the teachers and counsellors of the kings of Persia, skilled in the science and philosophy of their day.

In our understanding of the mysterious events surrounding the birth of Jesus, they form a strange contrast with the shepherds of Bethlehem. Between them these two sets of visitors to the infant Jesus embrace the Jew and the Gentile, the simple and the sophisticated, the rich and poor. Their coming reminds us that this was more than a turning-point in Hebrew history. Jesus is for the world.

Jesus was born in Bethlehem, in Judaea, in the days when Herod was king of the province. Not long after his birth there arrived from the east a party of astrologers making for Jerusalem and inquiring as they went: 'Where is the child born to be king of the Jews? For we saw his star in the east and we have come here to pay homage to him.'

When King Herod heard about this he was deeply perturbed, as indeed were all the other people living in Jerusalem. So he summoned all the Jewish scribes and chief priests together and asked them where 'Christ' should be born. Their reply was: 'In Bethlehem, in Judaea, for this is what the prophet wrote about the matter —

And thou Bethlehem, land of Judah,
Art in no wise least among the princes of Judah:
For out of thee shall come forth a governor,
Which shall be shepherd of my people Israel.'

Then Herod invited the wise men to meet him privately and found out from them the exact time when the star appeared. Then he sent them off to Bethlehem, saying, 'When you get there, search for this little child with the utmost care. And when you have found him, come back and tell me — so that I may go and worship him too.'

The wise men listened to the king and then went on their way to Bethlehem. And now the star, which they had seen in the east, went in front of them as they travelled until at last it shone immediately above the place where the little child lay. The sight of the star filled them with indescribable joy.

So they went into the house and saw the little child with his mother Mary. And they fell on their knees and worshipped him. Then they opened their treasures and presented him with gifts — gold, incense and myrrh.

Then, since they were warned in a dream not to return to Herod, they went back to their own country by a different route.

MATTHEW 2:1-12 *JBP*

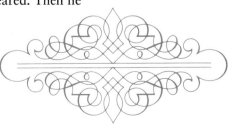

40

JORDAN'S RIVER

John the Baptizer (or John the Baptist) was a contemporary of Jesus, and distantly related to him. John was a man of the desert, called by God to a prophetic ministry 'to prepare the way of the Lord'. He preached the need to turn from sin, to confess the past and make a clean start. As men and women rose from the waters of the Jordan it was as though their past sins were washed away.

When John recognized Jesus among the crowds coming to him for baptism, he was taken aback. He saw in Jesus that 'Lord' whose coming he foretold in his own preaching. But Jesus set aside John's doubts and protests. By submitting to John's baptism (although himself with no sin) he identified himself with the whole human race. Here the beginning of his own public ministry is marked by the power of the Holy Spirit and the assurance of the Father's love to prepare him for all that lies ahead.

Jesus arrived at the Jordan from Galilee, and came to John to be baptized by him. John tried to dissuade him. 'Do you come to me?' he said; 'I need rather to be baptized by you.' Jesus replied, 'Let it be so for the present; we do well to conform in this way with all that God requires.' John then allowed him to come. After baptism Jesus came up out of the water at once, and at that moment heaven opened; he saw the Spirit of God descending like a dove to alight upon him; and a voice from heaven was heard saying, 'This is my Son, my Beloved, on whom my favour rests.'

MATTHEW 3:13-17 *NEB*

41

IN THE DESERT

Following his baptism, Jesus needed to be alone. For forty days he made his home in the desert wilderness of Judaea, hot and dusty and dry, treeless and silent. Here, in an account that could only have come from his own lips, he wrestled with the worst the devil could do to turn him aside from following his Father's call. He was tempted first to use his powers to prove his own identity; or to meet his own needs rather than those of others. More subtly, the devil went on to suggest that by one public act of spectacular miracle he could be assured of a great following. And when these failed, there was the final bribe: 'Take anything you choose — the kingdoms of the world and their magnificence — it can be all yours for a moment's homage.'

And to each temptation, Jesus replied with words from the Bible. Finally, foiled at least for the moment, the devil left him.

Then Jesus was led by the Spirit up into the desert, to be tempted by the devil. After a fast of forty days and nights he was very hungry.

'If you really are the Son of God,' said the tempter, coming to him, 'tell these stones to turn into loaves.'

Jesus answered, 'The scripture says "Man shall not live by bread alone, but by every word that proceedeth out of the mouth of God".'

Then the devil took him to the holy city, and set him on the highest ledge of the Temple. 'If you really are the Son of God,' he said, 'throw yourself down. For the scripture says —

He shall give his angels charge
   concerning thee:
And on their hands they shall bear thee up,
Lest haply thou dash thy foot against a stone.'

'Yes,' retorted Jesus, 'and the scripture also says "Thou shall not tempt the Lord thy God".'

Once again the devil took him to a very high mountain, and from there showed him all the kingdoms of the world and their magnificence. 'Everything there I will give you,' he said to him, 'if you will fall down and worship me.'

'Away with you, Satan!' replied Jesus, 'the scripture says,

Thou shalt worship the Lord thy God, and
   him only shalt thou serve.'

Then the devil let him alone, and angels came to him and took care of him.

MATTHEW 4:1-11 *JBP*

42

NICODEMUS

Pharisees were serious-minded religious leaders. As we know from the Gospels, they were not at all in favour of unauthorized new teachers — such as this Jesus of Nazareth, son of a local carpenter! But Nicodemus was an honest man, and in the miracles of Jesus, and in the refreshing vitality of his teaching, he found himself brought into a closer understanding of the God he sought to serve.

Did he come by night because he did not want his friends to see him visiting the lodging of this radical new preacher? At any rate he asked his questions, and was prepared to listen as Jesus spoke of a transformed relationship to God so new and life-changing that it could only be called a new birth: a new birth to a totally new life — spiritual, divine, eternal life.

This new life, the gift of God's love towards us, becomes ours as we put our trust in Jesus Christ, God's Son. And it is Christ 'lifted up' who brings us eternal life — Christ on his cross, who died to bear our sins and set us free.

We do not know what were the thoughts of this enquiring Pharisee as he walked homewards through the darkened streets. We do know, however, that when we meet him next, regardless of what his friends might think of him, he is ready to speak and act in support of Jesus.

There was a Jewish leader named Nicodemus, who belonged to the party of the Pharisees. One night he went to Jesus and said to him, 'Rabbi, we know that you are a teacher sent by God. No one could perform the miracles you are doing unless God were with him.'

Jesus answered, 'I am telling you the truth: no one can see the Kingdom of God unless he is born again.'

'How can a grown man be born again?' Nicodemus asked. 'He certainly cannot enter his mother's womb and be born a second time!'

'I am telling you the truth,' replied Jesus. 'No one can enter the Kingdom of God unless he is born of water and the Spirit. A person is born physically of human parents, but he is born spiritually of the Spirit. Do not be surprised because I tell you that you must all be born again. The wind blows wherever it wishes; you hear the sound it makes, but you do not know where it comes from or where it is going. It is like that with everyone who is born of the Spirit.'

'How can this be?' asked Nicodemus.

Jesus answered, 'You are a great teacher in Israel, and you don't know this? I am telling you the truth: we speak of what we know and report what we have seen, yet none of you is willing to accept our message. You do not believe me when I tell you about the things of this world; how will you ever believe me, then, when I tell you about the things of heaven? And no one has ever gone up to heaven except the Son of Man, who came down from heaven.'

As Moses lifted up the bronze snake on a pole in the desert, in the same way the Son of Man must be lifted up, so that everyone who believes in him may have eternal life. For God loved the world so much that he gave his only Son, so that everyone who believes in him may not die but have eternal life. For God did not send his Son into the world to be its judge, but to be its saviour.

JOHN 3:1-17 *GNB*

NEW TESTAMENT: THE LIFE OF JESUS

AT JACOB'S WELL

Jesus and his friends had been on the road since early morning, travelling north to Galilee. Their way led them through the territory of Samaria, whose people had a long-standing feud with the Jews, their neighbours. It was about midday when, hot and thirsty, Jesus sat down by Jacob's Well, and as he rested a woman came to draw water.

Starting from their shared experience of the moment, he speaks with the woman about 'living water', the new experience of God that lay at the heart of his own mission. But to receive this water of life means to come in all her need, hiding nothing, to God who is spirit, and truth. Neither holy place nor temple at Jerusalem, he tells her, is what really matters when we worship God. The Father seeks for worshippers who will draw near to him in sincerity of heart with faith and love.

There came a woman of Samaria to draw water. Jesus said to her, 'Give me a drink.' For his disciples had gone away into the city to buy food. The Samaritan woman said to him, 'How is it that you, a Jew, ask a drink of me, a woman of Samaria?' For Jews have no dealings with Samaritans. Jesus answered her, 'If you knew the gift of God, and who it is that is saying to you, "Give me a drink," you would have asked him, and he would have given you living water.' The woman said to him, 'Sir, you have nothing to draw with, and the well is deep; where do you get that living water? Are you greater than our father Jacob, who gave us the well, and drank from it himself, and his sons, and his cattle?' Jesus said to her, 'Every one who drinks of this water will thirst again, but whoever drinks of the water that I shall give him will never thirst; the water that I shall give him will become in him a spring of water welling up to eternal life.' The woman said to him, 'Sir, give me this water, that I may not thirst, nor come here to draw.'

Jesus said to her, 'Go, call your husband, and come here.' The woman answered him, 'I have no husband.' Jesus said to her, 'You are right in saying, "I have no husband"; for you have had five husbands, and he whom you now have is not your husband; this you said truly.' The woman said to him, 'Sir, I perceive that you are a prophet. Our fathers worshipped on this mountain; and you say that in Jerusalem is the place where men ought to worship.' Jesus said to her, 'Woman, believe me, the hour is coming when neither on this mountain nor in Jerusalem will you worship the Father. You worship what you do not know; we worship what we know, for salvation is from the Jews. But the hour is coming, and now is, when the true worshippers will worship the Father in spirit and truth, for such the Father seeks to worship him. God is spirit, and those who worship him must worship in spirit and truth.' The woman said to him, 'I know that Messiah is coming (he who is called Christ); when he comes, he will show us all things.' Jesus said to her, 'I who speak to you am he.'

JOHN 4:7-26 *RSV*

44

'FOLLOW ME'

The Sea of Galilee is a vast inland lake. In Jesus' day its shores were home to many families who made their living from it. At one time there were over 300 fishing boats at work.

No doubt these four young fishermen, Simon and Andrew, James and John, had heard Jesus preaching on previous occasions, and come to know and respect him. Their hearts were stirred by his message — and by the man he was. No doubt, too, he had taken his time, and thought and prayed, before inviting them to become part of his closest circle of disciples. But now 'the time has come'. He calls them to join his company and be his friends and followers. 'Repent' was his message to the crowd: 'Believe the good news of the gospel.' But to those who were ready to respond he goes on to give his personal call: 'Come, follow me.'

Jesus went into Galilee, proclaiming the good news of God. 'The time has come,' he said. 'The kingdom of God is near. Repent and believe the good news!'

As Jesus walked beside the Sea of Galilee, he saw Simon and his brother Andrew casting a net into the lake, for they were fishermen. 'Come, follow me,' Jesus said, 'and I will make you fishers of men.' At once they left their nets and followed him.

When he had gone a little farther, he saw James son of Zebedee and his brother John in a boat, preparing their nets. Without delay he called them, and they left their father Zebedee in the boat with the hired men and followed him.

MARK 1:14-20 *NIV*

46

SAVING FAITH

In the time of Jesus, Palestine was territory held by Rome; an army of occupation governed the country. In the Roman army a centurion commanded a hundred men (just as our word 'century' denotes a hundred years) — a sort of Company Sergeant-Major.

This centurion seems to have taken the trouble to learn something of the Jewish nation and their religion — and to have admired what he saw. He also recognized authority when he met it; and in all he had heard of Jesus he sensed that here was a man with an authority not unlike his own, whose orders would be obeyed without question. He had implicit faith that Jesus could and would command the healing of his servant — and that it would be accomplished.

Matthew tells us that in Jesus' home town of Nazareth, he did few miracles 'because of their unbelief'. By contrast, this believing Roman of Capernaum found his dying servant fully and completely healed.

45

TRUE HAPPINESS

Early in the ministry of Jesus there comes the 'Sermon on the Mount', recorded by Matthew. Luke's Gospel has a similar passage sometimes called the 'Sermon on the Plain' because Luke speaks of 'a level place'. Probably the disciples heard Jesus give this teaching many times over, to differing audiences in different places.

It has been called 'the perfect rule or pattern for Christian life', though describing a kind of person rather than offering a set of detailed regulations. These high principles of living belong to a life built upon love rather than law. For that reason the opening sayings are known as 'the Beatitudes' — and in our older translations they begin with the word 'blessed . . .' instead of 'happy'. It is not a word we use much now; but in some ways it conveys more of the meaning. Happiness is tied to circumstance; life may give it at one moment, and take it away the next. To be 'blessed' is to be in the hand of God and so, in the last resort, beyond the reach of human suffering and loss.

Happy are those who know they are spiritually
    poor;
  the Kingdom of heaven belongs to them!
Happy are those who mourn;
  God will comfort them!
Happy are those who are humble;
  they will receive what God has promised!
Happy are those whose greatest desire
    is to do what God requires;
  God will satisfy them fully!
Happy are those who are merciful to others;
  God will be merciful to them!
Happy are the pure in heart;
  they will see God!

Happy are those who work for peace;
  God will call them his children!
Happy are those who are persecuted
    because they do what God requires;
  the Kingdom of heaven belongs to them!
Happy are you when people insult you and persecute you and tell all kinds of evil lies against you because you are my followers. Be happy and glad, for a great reward is kept for you in heaven. This is how the prophets who lived before you were persecuted.

MATTHEW 5:3-12 GNB

When Jesus had finished these talks to the people, he came to Capernaum, where it happened that there was a man very seriously ill and in fact at the point of death. He was the slave of a centurion who thought very highly of him. When the centurion heard about Jesus, he sent some Jewish elders to him with the request that he would come and save his servant's life. When they came to Jesus, they urged him strongly to grant this request, saying that the centurion deserved to have this done for him. 'He loves our nation and has built us a synagogue out of his own pocket,' they said.

So Jesus went with them, but as he approached the house, the centurion sent some of his personal friends with the message,

'Don't trouble yourself, sir! I'm not important enough for you to come into my house — I didn't think I was fit to come to you in person. Just give the order, please, and my servant will recover. I am used to working under orders, and I have soldiers under me. I can say to one, "Go", and he goes, or I can say to another, "Come here", and he comes; or I can say to my slave, "Do this job", and he does it.'

These words amazed Jesus and he turned to the crowd who were following behind him, and said,

'I have never found faith like this anywhere, even in Israel!'

Then those who had been sent by the centurion returned to the house and found the slave perfectly well.

LUKE 7:1-10 JBP

47

THE GIFT OF LOVE

These few verses contain a story-within-a-story. The host at a dinner party is displeased that a woman of the streets should invade his house and make an exhibition of herself. By way of reply Jesus tells this story of two debtors. Its main thrust to Simon (as to us who read it) is 'If you had found the forgiveness this woman knows, you too would love me as much as she does'. Love comes from sins forgiven.

One of the Pharisees invited Jesus to a meal. When he arrived at the Pharisee's house and took his place at table, a woman came in, who had a bad name in the town. She had heard he was dining with the Pharisee and had brought with her an alabaster jar of ointment. She waited behind him at his feet, weeping, and her tears fell on his feet, and she wiped them away with her hair; then she covered his feet with kisses and anointed them with the ointment.

48

THE GROUND OF THE HEART

Though usually called the parable of the sower, this is really a parable of the different kinds of soil. Unlike most of Jesus' parables, we have his own interpretation of it in the following verses. There Jesus shares with his disciples one of the secrets of life in his kingdom, that what matters is that we approach him with an open and receptive heart.

Note too that 'the sower sows the word'. Like seeds, the words of Jesus contain a mysterious principle of life. In the good soil of a true and receptive heart they bear their fruit.

A sower went out to sow. And as he sowed, some seed fell along the path, and the birds came and devoured it. Other seed fell on rocky ground, where it had not much soil, and immediately it sprang up, since it had no depth of soil; and when the sun rose it was scorched, and since it had no root it withered away. Other seed fell among thorns and the thorns grew up and choked it, and it yielded no grain. And other seeds fell into good soil and brought forth grain, growing up and increasing and yielding thirtyfold and sixtyfold and a hundredfold.' And he said, 'He who has ears to hear, let him hear.'

And when he was alone, those who were about him with the twelve asked him concerning the parables. And he said to them, 'To you has been given the secret of the kingdom of God, but for those outside everything is in parables; so that they may indeed see but not perceive, and may indeed hear but not understand; lest they should turn again, and be forgiven.' And he said to them, 'Do you not understand this parable? How then will you understand all the parables? The sower sows the word. And these are the ones along the path, where the word is sown; when they hear, Satan immediately comes and takes away the word which is sown in them. And these in like manner are the ones sown upon rocky ground, who, when they hear the word, immediately receive it with joy; and they have no root in themselves, but endure for a while; then, when tribulation or persecution arises on account of the word, immediately they

When the Pharisee who had invited him saw this, he said to himself, 'If this man were a prophet, he would know who this woman is that is touching him and what a bad name she has.' Then Jesus took him up and said, 'Simon, I have something to say to you.' 'Speak, Master' was the reply. 'There was once a creditor who had two men in his debt; one owed him five hundred denarii, the other fifty. They were unable to pay, so he pardoned them both. Which of them will love him more?' 'The one who was pardoned more, I suppose,' answered Simon. Jesus said, 'You are right.'

Then he turned to the woman. 'Simon,' he said 'you see this woman? I came into your house, and you poured no water over my feet, but she has poured out her tears over my feet and wiped them away with her hair. You gave me no kiss, but she has been covering my feet with kisses ever since I came in. You did not anoint my head with oil, but she has anointed my feet with ointment. For this reason I tell you that her sins, her many sins, must have been forgiven her, or she would not have shown such great love. It is the man who is forgiven little who shows little love.' Then he said to her, 'Your sins are forgiven.' Those who were with him at table began to say to themselves, 'Who is this man, that he even forgives sins?' But he said to the woman, 'Your faith has saved you; go in peace.'

LUKE 7:36-50 *JB*

fall away. And others are the ones sown among thorns; they are those who hear the word, but the cares of the world, and the delight in riches, and the desire for other things, enter in and choke the word, and it proves unfruitful. But those that were sown upon the good soil are the ones who hear the word and accept it and bear fruit, thirtyfold and sixtyfold and a hundredfold.'

MARK 4:3-20 *RSV*

49

WIND AND STORM

Jesus and his friends were used to boats. The first of his disciples came from fishing families along the shores of the Sea of Galilee, a lake notorious for its sudden squalls. Mark draws a vivid picture of Jesus, exhausted from a whole day's travelling and teaching, sleeping soundly while the storm rises.

And Mark has a purpose behind the picture he provides. A recurring theme of his Gospel is to provoke the question here asked by the disciples. In the face of their Master's power even over the wind and wave they say to one another: 'Who can this be?'

Seriously to ask that question is to be on the way to finding the answer.

That day, in the evening, Jesus said to them, 'Let us cross over to the other side of the lake.' So they left the crowd and took him with them in the boat where he had been sitting; and there were other boats accompanying him. A heavy squall came on and the waves broke over the boat until it was all but swamped. Now he was in the stern asleep on a cushion; they roused him and said, 'Master, we are sinking! Do you not care?' He awoke, rebuked the wind, and said to the sea, 'Hush! Be still!' The wind dropped and there was a dead calm. He said to them, 'Why are you such cowards? Have you no faith even now?' They were awestruck and said to one another, 'Who can this be? Even the wind and the sea obey him.'

MARK 4:35-41 *NEB*

THE FEEDING OF THE FIVE THOUSAND

This story must have made a great impression on the writers of the Gospels. Matthew, Mark, Luke and John all record it. John tells us that it was near the time of the Passover — which means it was springtime; and he alone mentions the unnamed boy whose loaves (the equivalent of little barley rolls) and dried fish fed 5,000 people.

In John's Gospel, the miracles are often called signs — acts of deep meaning and significance, something much more than mere wonders. And so behind this simple story we see Christ's compassion for the hungry, whether of body or of spirit; and are reminded of his power to take what may be offered to him, however inadequate, and make of it enough to meet all needs — with some to spare.

Some time later Jesus withdrew to the farther shore of the Sea of Galilee (or Tiberias), and a large crowd of people followed who had seen the signs he performed in healing the sick. Then Jesus went up the hillside and sat down with his disciples. It was near the time of Passover, the great Jewish festival. Raising his eyes and seeing a large crowd coming towards him, Jesus said to Philip, 'Where are we to buy bread to feed these people?' This he said to test him; Jesus himself knew what he meant to do. Philip replied, 'Twenty pounds would not buy enough bread for every one of them to have a little.' One of his disciples, Andrew, the brother of Simon Peter, said to him, 'There is a boy here who has five barley loaves and two fishes; but what is that among so many?' Jesus said, 'Make the people sit down.' There was plenty of grass there, so the men sat down, about five thousand of them. Then Jesus took the loaves, gave thanks, and distributed them to the people as they sat there. He did the same with the fishes, and they had as much as they wanted. When everyone had had enough, he said to his disciples, 'Collect the pieces left over, so that nothing may be lost.' This they did, and filled twelve baskets with the pieces left uneaten of the five barley loaves.

When the people saw the sign Jesus had performed, the word went round, 'Surely this must be the prophet that was to come into the world.'

JOHN 6:1-14 *NEB*

51

'YOU ARE THE CHRIST!'

For centuries the Jews had been waiting for God's Messiah, the Anointed One, who would lead them to freedom and usher in a new age. Under Roman occupation these hopes became ever more vivid — it would soon be asked of any new popular leader whether he might not at last be God's Messiah.

But Jesus was different. No one who listened to his teaching could believe that he saw his mission as leading Israel to freedom from the Roman yoke. He talked of a kingdom — but a kingdom 'not of this world'.

He had been careful not to encourage speculation about his identity. Those whom he healed were instructed not to make it public. Evil spirits whom he exorcized, and who knew his real identity, were condemned to silence. But here at Caesarea Philippi, resting together on their journey, Jesus asks what the crowds are saying about him; and then what his own followers believe. When Peter, ever impetuous, bursts out with his confession of faith, Jesus is ready to begin to prepare the twelve disciples for his suffering and death.

When Jesus came to the region of Caesarea Philippi, he asked his disciples, 'Who do people say the Son of Man is?'

They replied, 'Some say John the Baptist; others say Elijah; and still others, Jeremiah or one of the prophets.'

'But what about you?' he asked. 'Who do you say I am?'

Simon Peter answered, 'You are the Christ, the Son of the living God.'

Jesus replied, 'Blessed are you, Simon son of Jonah, for this was not revealed to you by man, but by my Father in heaven. And I tell you that you are Peter, and on this rock I will build my church, and the gates of Hades will not overcome it. I will give you the keys of the kingdom of heaven; whatever you bind on earth will be bound in heaven, and whatever you loose on earth will be loosed in heaven.' Then he warned his disciples not to tell anyone that he was the Christ.

From that time on Jesus began to explain to his disciples that he must go to Jerusalem and suffer many things at the hands of the elders, chief priests and teachers of the law, and that he must be killed and on the third day be raised to life.

Peter took him aside and began to rebuke him. 'Never, Lord!' he said. 'This shall never happen to you!'

Jesus turned and said to Peter, 'Get behind me, Satan! You are a stumbling-block to me; you do not have in mind the things of God, but the things of men.'

Then Jesus said to his disciples, 'If anyone would come after me, he must deny himself and take up his cross and follow me. For whoever wants to save his life will lose it, but whoever loses his life for me will find it.'

MATTHEW 16:13-25 *NIV*

52

'MY SON, MY CHOSEN'

Jesus often prayed in the open air, choosing some lonely place among the hills where he could be undisturbed. Here, with Peter and James and John, he shares a unique experience. It is as though the boundary between our world and the unseen world of spiritual reality parted for a moment — almost as though a door was opened in heaven. There on that remote hillside, the three disciples of his innermost circle were allowed a glimpse of Jesus, not as the Man of Galilee but as the Lord of Glory.

Moses and Elijah, representatives of God's ancient covenant with Israel, are there with him. They talk together of God's plan to bring his wayward people back into relationship with himself. This plan, foreshadowed in the Old Testament, will be completed by Jesus' suffering on the cross. And as Jesus prepares himself for this final obedience — the finishing of the work his Father committed to him — there comes again (as at his baptism) the voice of God from within the cloud: 'This is my Son, my Chosen'.

Jesus took Peter, John, and James with him and went up into the hills to pray. And while he was praying the appearance of his face changed and his clothes became dazzling white. Suddenly there were two men talking with him; these were Moses and Elijah, who appeared in glory and spoke of his departure, the destiny he was to fulfil in Jerusalem. Meanwhile Peter and his companions had been in a deep sleep; but when they awoke, they saw his glory and the two men who stood beside him. And as these were moving away from Jesus, Peter said to him, 'Master, how good it is that we are here! Shall we make three shelters, one for you, one for Moses, and one for Elijah?'; but he spoke without knowing what he was saying. The words were still on his lips, when there came a cloud which cast a shadow over them; they were afraid as they entered the cloud, and from it came a voice: 'This is my Son, my Chosen; listen to him.'

LUKE 9:28-35 *NEB*

53

THE GOOD SHEPHERD

In the Old Testament, God himself is 'the Shepherd of Israel'. Here Jesus likens himself to the shepherd of a flock. At night such a shepherd would lead his sheep into a stone-walled enclosure with a single entrance. When they were all safely in, he himself would lie down across the entrance, and become 'the door of the sheep'. So Jesus claims to be 'the door', the way into the fold through whom new and abundant life begins.

At the end of this passage there is a reminder that in everything which follows, Jesus is in control. No one — no priest or governor, Jewish rabble or Roman soldier — *no one* takes his life from him. He chooses to lay it down. The Good Shepherd willingly gives his life for the sheep.

'Truly, truly, I say to you, I am the door of the sheep. All who came before me are thieves and robbers; but the sheep did not heed them. I am the door; if any one enters by me, he will be saved, and will go in and out and find pasture. The thief comes only to steal and kill and destroy; I came that they may have life, and have it abundantly. I am the good shepherd. The good shepherd lays down his life for the sheep. He who is a hireling and not a shepherd, whose own the sheep are not, sees the wolf coming and leaves the sheep and flees; and the wolf snatches them and scatters them. He flees because he is a hireling and cares nothing for the sheep. I am the good shepherd; I know my own and my own know me, as the Father knows me and I know the Father; and I lay down my life for the sheep. And I have other sheep, that are not of this fold; I must bring them also, and they will heed my voice. So there shall be one flock, one shepherd. For this reason the Father loves me, because I lay down my life, that I may take it again. No one takes it from me, but I lay it down of my own accord. I have power to lay it down, and I have power to take it again; this charge I have received from my Father.'

JOHN 10:7-18 *RSV*

54

'WHO IS MY NEIGHBOUR?'

Even today, when we want to describe a man or woman who has come to our rescue we call them 'a good Samaritan'. When Jesus told this story, the Jews looked down on the Samaritans; they were a despised people. In the punch-line at the end, when Jesus asked the teacher of the Law to answer his own question and say which of these three characters deserved the name 'neighbour', he could not bring himself to say 'the Samaritan'.

A teacher of the Law came up and tried to trap Jesus. 'Teacher,' he asked, 'what must I do to receive eternal life?'

Jesus answered him, 'What do the Scriptures say? How do you interpret them?'

The man answered, '"Love the Lord your God with all your heart, with all your soul, with all your strength, and with all your mind"; and "Love your neighbour as you love yourself."'

'You are right,' Jesus replied, 'do this and you will live.'

But the teacher of the Law wanted to justify himself, so he asked Jesus, 'Who is my neighbour?'

Jesus answered, 'There was once a man who was going down from Jerusalem to Jericho when robbers attacked him, stripped him, and beat him up, leaving him half dead. It so happened that a priest was going down that road; but when he saw the man, he walked on by, on the other side. In the same way a Levite also came along, went over and looked at the man, and then walked on by, on the other side. But a Samaritan who was travelling that way came upon the man, and when he saw him, his heart was filled with pity. He went over to him, poured oil and wine on his wounds and bandaged them; then he put the man on his own animal and took him to an inn, where he took care of him. The next day he took out two silver coins and gave them to the innkeeper. "Take care of him," he told the innkeeper, "and when I come back this way, I will pay you whatever else you spend on him."'

And Jesus concluded, 'In your opinion, which one of these three acted like a neighbour towards the man attacked by the robbers?'

The teacher of the Law answered, 'The one who was kind to him.'

Jesus replied, 'You go, then, and do the same.'

LUKE 10:25-37 *GNB*

55

THE PATTERN PRAYER

Jesus only taught one prayer to his disciples, as far as we have any record. We therefore call it 'the Lord's Prayer'. Down all the Christian centuries, it has been the one prayer almost every believer knows by heart. The older version, known to millions, is modelled on this translation, substituting the word 'trespasses' (straying from the straight path) for 'debts' (wrongs done to God or man).

It has been called a 'pattern' because of the order in which it leads us to bring our requests to a heavenly Father. We pray first about his business — his name, his kingdom, his will. Only then do we ask for ourselves, for the needs of the day, and for his forgiveness of its faults, remembering that it is useless to ask forgiveness, if we ourselves nourish grudges and resentments, and are unwilling to forgive. Finally we pray for God's direction and for his protection — finishing with a burst of praise.

But when ye pray, use not vain repetitions, as the heathen do: for they think that they shall be heard for their much speaking.

Be not ye therefore like unto them: for your Father knoweth what things ye have need of, before ye ask him.

After this manner therefore pray ye: Our Father which art in heaven, Hallowed be thy name.

Thy kingdom come. Thy will be done in earth, as it is in heaven.

Give us this day our daily bread.

And forgive us our debts, as we forgive our debtors.

And lead us not into temptation, but deliver us from evil: For thine is the kingdom, and the power, and the glory, for ever. Amen.

MATTHEW 6:7-13 KJV

56

THE YOUNGER SON

This must be among the most famous of all the stories and parables Jesus told. It is the third of a set of three — about a straying sheep, a missing coin, and finally a lost son. It is a most vivid illustration, in narrative terms, of what we mean when we say that God is love. Short though the story is, the character of this father is wonderfully drawn for us. He is just and open-handed with his family. He is the kind of man an erring son can face returning to. This father's eyes are never far from the road on which he hopes one day to see his son come home. He hears his son's confession and apology, but cuts it short. Notice what the son intended to say, and never managed to. The father wants his *son*, not another servant for his farm.

And what does this wayward son return to? A well-deserved lecture? Black looks and disapproving faces? Repeated reminders of his foolishness and the error of his ways? Not at all! There is a feast, a celebration! As Jesus has reminded his hearers twice already in this chapter, there is joy in heaven over a sinner who returns home.

Once there was a man who had two sons. The younger one said to his father, 'Father, give me my share of the property that will come to me.' So he divided up his property between the two of them. Before very long, the younger son collected all his belongings and went off to a foreign land, where he squandered his wealth in the wildest extravagance. And when he had run through all his money, a terrible famine arose in that country, and he began to feel the pinch. Then he went and hired himself out to one of the citizens of that country who sent him out into the fields to feed the pigs. He got to the point of longing to stuff himself with the food the pigs were eating, and not a soul gave him anything. Then he came to his senses and cried aloud, 'Why, dozens of my father's hired men have got more food than they can eat and here am I dying of hunger! I will get up and go back to my father, and I will say to him, "Father, I have done wrong in the sight of Heaven and in your eyes. I don't deserve to be called your son any more. Please take me on as one of your hired men."' So he got up and went to his father. But while he was still some distance off, his father saw him and his heart went out to him, and he ran and fell on his neck and kissed him. But his son said, 'Father, I have done wrong in the sight of Heaven and in your eyes. I don't deserve to be called your son any more . . . ' 'Hurry!' called out his father to the servants, 'fetch the best clothes and put them on him! Put a ring on his finger and shoes on his feet, and get that calf we've fattened and kill it, and we will have a feast and a celebration! For this is my son — I thought he was dead, and he's alive again. I thought I had lost him, and he's found!'

LUKE 15:11-24 *JBP*

'THE RESURRECTION AND THE LIFE'

NEW TESTAMENT: THE LIFE OF JESUS

At Bethany, a village on the outskirts of Jerusalem, there lived a family who were friends of Jesus. Martha and Mary were sisters, Lazarus their brother. Jesus sometimes stayed at their home.

Lazarus fell sick while Jesus was travelling in the north. Word was sent for him to come urgently, but he delayed his departure, fully aware that by the time he got to Bethany, Lazarus would be dead. Indeed, Jesus told his disciples that for their sakes he was glad that it was in his absence that Lazarus had died, because in this way it would bring glory to God. Naturally enough, they quite failed to understand. But Jesus had a demonstration for them all, a lesson in faith before he too was dead and buried, to show that death itself was subject to his word of power.

When Martha heard that Jesus was coming, she went out to meet him, but Mary stayed at home.

'Lord,' Martha said to Jesus, 'if you had been here, my brother would not have died. But I know that even now God will give you whatever you ask.'

Jesus said to her, 'Your brother will rise again.'

Martha answered, 'I know he will rise again in the resurrection at the last day.'

Jesus said to her, 'I am the resurrection and the life. He who believes in me will live, even though he dies; and whoever lives and believes in me will never die. Do you believe this?'

'Yes, Lord,' she told him. 'I believe that you are the Christ, the Son of God, who was to come into the world.'

And after she had said this, she went back and called her sister Mary aside. 'The Teacher is here,' she said, 'and is asking for you.' When Mary heard this, she got up quickly and went to him. Now Jesus had not yet entered the village, but was still at the place where Martha had met him. When the Jews who had been with Mary in the house, comforting her, noticed how quickly she got up and went out, they followed her, supposing she was going to the tomb to mourn there.

When Mary reached the place where Jesus was and saw him, she fell at his feet and said, 'Lord, if you had been here, my brother would not have died.'

When Jesus saw her weeping, and the Jews who had come along with her also weeping, he was deeply moved in spirit and troubled. 'Where have you laid him?' he asked.

'Come and see, Lord,' they replied.

Jesus wept.

Then the Jews said, 'See how he loved him!'

But some of them said, 'Could not he who opened the eyes of the blind man have kept this man from dying?'

Jesus, once more deeply moved, came to the tomb. It was a cave with a stone laid across the entrance. 'Take away the stone,' he said.

'But, Lord,' said Martha, the sister of the dead man, 'by this time there is a bad odour, for he has been there four days.'

Then Jesus said, 'Did I not tell you that if you believed, you would see the glory of God?'

So they took away the stone. Then Jesus looked up and said, 'Father, I thank you that you have heard me. I knew that you always hear me, but I said this for the benefit of the people standing here, that they may believe that you sent me.'

When he had said this, Jesus called in a loud voice, 'Lazarus, come out!' The dead man came out, his hands and feet wrapped with strips of linen, and a cloth around his face.

Jesus said to them, 'Take off the grave clothes and let him go.'

JOHN 11:20-44 *NIV*

58

THE KING COMES!

Jesus is on his way to Jerusalem for the Passover — and for the finishing of his work. Word had got about that this strange teacher from Galilee had raised a dead man to life. Once again there is a surge of Messianic expectation. An excited crowd turns out to welcome Jesus to Jerusalem. But this is no conquering king, riding on a white charger at the head of a triumphant army of liberation! By the end of the day, popular expectation is disillusioned; this is not the kind of king they had been hoping for. Soon, probably, the same voices that had called 'Hosanna' would be shouting 'Crucify him! Crucify him!'

But the religious leaders took note of the disturbance. They were growing impatient and afraid. The Roman government would not tolerate a civic disturbance. What they most wanted was some means of silencing Jesus out of the public eye.

The next day a great crowd who had come to the feast heard that Jesus was coming to Jerusalem. So they took branches of palm trees and went out to meet him, crying, 'Hosanna! Blessed be he who comes in the name of the Lord, even the King of Israel!' And Jesus found a young ass and sat upon it; as it is written,

'Fear not, daughter of Zion;
behold thy king is coming,
sitting on an ass's colt!'

His disciples did not understand this at first; but when Jesus was glorified, then they remembered that this had been written of him and had been done to him. The crowd that had been with him when he called Lazarus out of the tomb and raised him from the dead bore witness. The reason why the crowd went to meet him was that they heard he had done this sign. The Pharisees then said to one another, 'You see that you can do nothing; look, the world has gone after him.'

JOHN 12:12-19 *RSV*

59

THE FEAST OF PASSOVER

Ever since their great deliverance from Egypt under Moses, the Jews had faithfully kept the Passover. Some of them keep it still. Jerusalem was therefore crowded to capacity with pilgrims who had come up, like Jesus and his disciples, to keep the feast.

It is clear to Jesus that his time is running out. Judas is already in touch with the authorities, offering them a way to take Jesus prisoner with the least possible disturbance. But before that, there are things to be said and done at this final last Passover supper. Jesus makes his arrangements so that, for the evening at least, he and his closest followers will be alone together for the last time before his death and burial.

Now the Feast of Unleavened Bread, called the Passover, was approaching, and the chief priests and the teachers of the law were looking for some way to get rid of Jesus, for they were afraid of the people. Then Satan entered Judas, called Iscariot, one of the Twelve. And Judas went to the chief priests and the officers of the temple guard and discussed with them how he might betray Jesus. They were delighted and agreed to give him money. He consented, and watched for an opportunity to hand Jesus over to them when no crowd was present.

Then came the day of Unleavened Bread on which the Passover lamb had to be sacrificed. Jesus sent Peter and John, saying, 'Go and make preparations for us to eat the Passover.'

'Where do you want us to prepare for it?' they asked.

He replied, 'As you enter the city, a man carrying a jar of water will meet you. Follow him to the house that he enters, and say to the owner of the house, "The Teacher asks: Where is the guest room, where I may eat the Passover with my disciples?" He will show you a large upper room, all furnished. Make preparations there.'

They left and found things just as Jesus had told them. So they prepared the Passover.

LUKE 22:1-13 *NIV*

60

THE LAST SUPPER

Libraries have been written without exhausting the meaning of this last meal together. Here, in symbolic acts, Jesus breaks the bread and pours the wine, just as on the following day his body will be broken on the cross, and his blood spilled.

But this cup of wine is called 'my blood of the covenant'. As the disciples drink it (and as Christ's disciples have done so ever since, in obedience to his words) it marks for them a share in that new covenant, in all the benefits of Christ's death for sinners, and in the assurance of his resurrection.

Now as they were eating, Jesus took bread, and blessed, and broke it, and gave it to the disciples and said, 'Take, eat; this is my body.' And he took a cup, and when he had given thanks he gave it to them, saying, 'Drink of it, all of you; for this is my blood of the covenant, which is poured out for many for the forgiveness of sins. I tell you I shall not drink again of this fruit of the vine until that day when I drink it new with you in my Father's kingdom.'

And when they had sung a hymn, they went out to the Mount of Olives. Then Jesus said to them, 'You will all fall away because of me this night; for it is written, "I will strike the shepherd, and the sheep of the flock will be scattered." But after I am raised up, I will go before you to Galilee.' Peter declared to him, 'Though they all fall away because of you, I will never fall away.' Jesus said to him, 'Truly, I say to you, this very night, before the cock crows, you will deny me three times.' Peter said to him, 'Even if I must die with you, I will not deny you.' And so said all the disciples.

MATTHEW 26:26-35 *RSV*

61

GETHSEMANE

Gethsemane was an olive garden, deserted that night, and lit only by the paschal moon. Here, in the company of his friends and yet removed a little from them, Jesus faces what lies before him.

What begins as a prayer for himself becomes by the end a prayer that his Father's purposes will be fulfilled — the same prayer that once before he taught these slumbering disciples: 'Thy will be done.'

It was an ideal place for the betrayal. A considerable force seems to have been mustered. Jesus surrenders himself into their hands, just as he had foretold beforehand in his teaching: 'No man takes my life from me. I lay it down of my own accord.'

After a brief and half-hearted struggle, Jesus is alone in the power of his accusers.

Jesus then came with his disciples to a place called Gethsemane. He said to them, 'Sit here while I go over there to pray.' He took with him Peter and the two sons of Zebedee. Anguish and dismay came over him, and he said to them, 'My heart is ready to break with grief. Stop here, and stay awake with me.' He went on a little, fell on his face in prayer, and said, 'My Father, if it is possible, let this cup pass me by. Yet not as I will, but as thou wilt.'

He came to the disciples and found them asleep; and he said to Peter, 'What! Could none of you stay awake with me one hour? Stay awake, and pray that you may be spared the test. The spirit is willing, but the flesh is weak.'

He went away a second time, and prayed: 'My Father, if it is not possible for this cup to pass me by without my drinking it, thy will be done.' He came again and found them asleep, for their eyes were heavy. So he left them and went away again; and he prayed the third time, using the same words as before.

Then he came to the disciples and said to them, 'Still sleeping? Still taking your ease? The hour has come! The Son of Man is betrayed to sinful men. Up, let us go forward, the traitor is upon us.'

While he was still speaking, Judas, one of the Twelve, appeared; with him was a great crowd armed with swords and cudgels, sent by the chief priests and the elders of the nation. The traitor gave them this sign: 'The one I kiss is your man; seize him'; and, stepping forward at once, he said, 'Hail, Rabbi!', and kissed him. Jesus replied, 'Friend, do what you are here to do.' They then came forward, seized Jesus, and held him fast.

At that moment one of those with Jesus reached for his sword and drew it, and he struck at the High Priest's servant and cut off his ear. But Jesus said to him, 'Put up your sword. All who take the sword die by the sword. Do you suppose that I cannot appeal to my Father, who would at once send to my aid more than twelve legions of angels? But how then could the scriptures be fulfilled, which say that this must be?'

At the same time Jesus spoke to the crowd: 'Do you take me for a bandit, that you have come out with swords and cudgels to arrest me? Day after day I sat teaching in the temple, and you did not lay hands on me. But this has all happened to fulfil what the prophets wrote.'

Then the disciples all deserted him and ran away.

MATTHEW 26:36-56 *NEB*

62

IN THE HIGH PRIEST'S HOUSE

Sitting at supper, Simon Peter had protested his total loyalty to Jesus. 'I am ready to go with you to prison or to death' he had said, conscious that trouble with the authorities could not be far away. In his reply, Jesus warned Peter that before the dawn broke, at cock-crow the following day, Peter would three times over have denied all knowledge of him.

And so it happened. One lie leads to another.

It did not take a police enquiry, only a fireside conversation. The question came, not from an official but from a servant, not even from one of the men but from a maid of the household. One can imagine Jesus undergoing cross-examination in one of the rooms — perhaps an upper room — open to the central courtyard; and, at the sound of the first cock crowing, turning to look at Simon Peter in the bitter light of dawn.

63

BEFORE PILATE

It was 1961 before the first archaeological evidence was unearthed about Pontius Pilate, on a stone discovered at Caesarea. But his name has been a household word in Christian families for almost twenty centuries, remembered for one thing only: that Jesus Christ was 'crucified under Pontius Pilate'.

The priests and Jewish authorities had no power of execution. That was reserved for the Roman governor. So, after a night of interrogation and examination by the priests, Jesus was brought at first light to the governor's palace.

Mark in his account omits one telling incident preserved by Matthew: that when Pilate failed in his attempt to secure for Jesus the free pardon traditionally offered to one prisoner at festival-time, he called for a bowl of water and ceremonially washed his hands before the crowd. He told them, 'I take no responsibility for the death of this man.' History has judged differently.

The moment daylight came the chief priests called together a meeting of elders, scribes and members of the whole council, bound Jesus and took him off and handed him over to Pilate. Pilate asked him straight out,

'Well, you — *are* you the king of the Jews?'

'Yes, I am,' he replied.

The chief priests brought many accusations. So Pilate questioned him again,

'Have you nothing to say? Listen to all their accusations!'

But Jesus made no further answer — to Pilate's astonishment.

Now it was Pilate's custom at festival-time to release a prisoner — anyone they asked for. There was in the prison at the time, with some other rioters who had committed murder in a recent outbreak, a man called Barabbas. The crowd surged forward and began to demand

They arrested Jesus and took him away into the house of the High Priest; and Peter followed at a distance. A fire had been lit in the centre of the courtyard, and Peter joined those who were sitting round it. When one of the servant-girls saw him sitting there at the fire, she looked straight at him and said, 'This man too was with Jesus!'

But Peter denied it, 'Woman, I don't even know him!'

After a little while a man noticed Peter and said, 'You are one of them, too!'

But Peter answered, 'Man, I am not!'

And about an hour later another man insisted strongly, 'There isn't any doubt that this man was with Jesus, because he also is a Galilean!'

But Peter answered, 'Man, I don't know what you are talking about!'

At once, while he was still speaking, a cock crowed. The Lord turned round and looked straight at Peter, and Peter remembered that the Lord had said to him, 'Before the cock crows tonight, you will say three times that you do not know me.' Peter went out and wept bitterly.

LUKE 22:54-62 *GNB*

that Pilate should do what he usually did for them. So he spoke to them,

'Do you want me to set free the king of the Jews for you?'

For he knew perfectly well that the chief priests had handed Jesus over to him through sheer malice. But the chief priests worked upon the crowd to get them to demand Barabbas' release instead. So Pilate addressed them once more,

'Then what am I to do with the man whom you call the king of the Jews?'

They shouted back,

'Crucify him!'

But Pilate replied,

'Why, what crime has he committed?'

But their voices rose to a roar,

'Crucify him!'

And as Pilate wanted to satisfy the crowd, he set Barabbas free for them, and after having Jesus flogged handed him over to be crucified.

Then the soldiers marched him away inside the courtyard of the governor's residence and called their whole company together. They dressed Jesus in a purple robe, and twisting some thorn-twigs into a crown, they put it on his head. Then they began to greet him,

'Hail, your majesty — king of the Jews!'

They hit him on the head with a stick and spat at him, and then bowed low before him on bended knee. And when they had finished their fun with him, they took off the purple cloak and dressed him again in his own clothes. Then they led him outside to crucify him.

MARK 15:1-20 *JBP*

64

THE CROSS OF CALVARY

The writers of the Gospels are reticent about the physical horrors of crucifixion. It was in fact a death by torture, beginning with the terrible flogging (some men died under it, most lost consciousness) and continuing through the cruel horse-play of the Jerusalem garrison. Here was a man who set himself up to be a king, they thought, another wandering prophet with delusions of grandeur inciting the city to riot. It was the custom for the charge against the condemned man to be nailed to the cross above his head. And so the Romans wrote with tongue in cheek, partly as an insult to a subject people they despised, 'This is Jesus the king of the Jews.'

Pilate's soldiers then took Jesus into the Governor's headquarters, where they collected the whole company round him. They stripped him and dressed him in a scarlet mantle; and plaiting a crown of thorns they placed it on his head, with a cane in his right hand. Falling on their knees before him they jeered at him: 'Hail, King of the Jews!' They spat on him, and used the cane to beat him about the head. When they had finished their mockery, they took off the mantle and dressed him in his own clothes.

Then they led him away to be crucified. On their way out they met a man from Cyrene, Simon by name, and pressed him into service to carry his cross.

So they came to a place called Golgotha (which means 'Place of a skull') and there he was offered a draught of wine mixed with gall; but when he had tasted it he would not drink.

After fastening him to the cross they divided his clothes among them by casting lots, and then sat down there to keep watch. Over his head was placed the inscription giving the charge: 'This is Jesus the king of the Jews.'

MATTHEW 27:27-37 *NEB*

65

THE DEATH OF JESUS

Jesus was crucified at 9 o'clock in the morning and died at about 3 o'clock in the afternoon. Each of the Gospel writers tells the story from his own standpoint, selecting from among a host of incidents. No one account can do justice to this event. The cry recorded here in Aramaic is a direct quotation from Psalm 22. For six hours Jesus hung helpless, bearing there the sin of the world, pictured in the unnatural darkness beginning at midday. No one can imagine or enter into that experience. But a clue comes in the words of St Paul to the church at Corinth: 'God caused Christ, who himself knew nothing of sin, actually to *be* sin for our sakes, so that in Christ we might be made good with the goodness of God.'

Two bandits were crucified with him, one on his right and the other on his left.

The passers-by hurled abuse at him: they wagged their heads and cried, 'You would pull the temple down, would you, and build it in three days? Come down from the cross and save yourself, if you are indeed the Son of God.' So too the chief priests with the lawyers and elders mocked at him: 'He saved others,' they said, 'but he cannot save himself. King of Israel, indeed! Let him come down now from the cross, and then we will believe him. Did he trust in God? Let God rescue him, if he wants him — for he said he was God's Son.' Even the bandits who were crucified with him taunted him in the same way.

From midday a darkness fell over the whole land, which lasted until three in the afternoon; and about three Jesus cried aloud, '*Eli, Eli, lema sabachthani?*', which means, 'My God, my God, why hast thou forsaken me?' Some of the bystanders, on hearing this, said, 'He is calling Elijah.' One of them ran at once and fetched a sponge, which he soaked in sour wine, and held it to his lips on the end of a cane. But the others said, 'Let us see if Elijah will come to save him.'

Jesus again gave a loud cry, and breathed his last. At that moment the curtain of the temple was torn in two from top to bottom. There was an earthquake, the rocks split and the graves opened, and many of God's saints were raised from sleep; and coming out of their graves after his resurrection they entered the Holy City, where many saw them. And when the centurion and his men who were keeping watch over Jesus saw the earthquake and all that was happening, they were filled with awe, and they said, 'Truly this man was a son of God.'

MATTHEW 27:38-54 *NEB*

66

THE GARDEN TOMB

Jesus was crucified on a Friday — 'Good Friday' we call it, for on that day Jesus finished the work he came to do, the redeeming of a sinful world. In Jewish reckoning the next day was the Sabbath. The body was therefore hurriedly taken down, wrapped in spices, and temporarily laid to rest in a borrowed grave. Once the Sabbath was over his sorrowing friends planned to return and finish preparing the body for its final burial. Meanwhile the rock-hewn tomb was closed with a great stone.

Matthew tells us that the chief priests secured from Pontius Pilate a military guard to seal the entrance and keep watch. They knew that Jesus had spoken of his resurrection: and wanted to make sure that no one could come and steal the body, and so lend colour (perhaps for political purposes) to any story of his rising from the dead.

After this, Joseph of Arimathaea, who was a disciple of Jesus — though a secret one because he was afraid of the Jews — asked Pilate to let him remove the body of Jesus. Pilate gave permission, so they came and took it away. Nicodemus came as well — the same one who had first come to Jesus at night-time — and he brought a mixture of myrrh and aloes, weighing about a hundred pounds. They took the body of Jesus and wrapped it with the spices in linen cloths, following the Jewish burial custom. At the place where he had been crucified there was a garden, and in this garden a new tomb in which no one had yet been buried. Since it was the Jewish Day of Preparation and the tomb was near at hand, they laid Jesus there.

JOHN 19:38-42 *JB*

67

THE FIRST DAY OF THE WEEK

Three women made their way before dawn to the tomb to complete the preparation of Jesus' body for burial. They began to ask themselves how they would move the stone. Perhaps they had set off assuming that their combined strength would be enough — and then as they drew nearer began to have doubts.

They need not have worried. The stone was rolled back and the tomb empty. The angel gives them his astonishing message and urges them to look into the cave and see for themselves. There, so John tells us, the linen wrappings were lying 'and the napkin which had been over his head, not lying with the wrappings but rolled together in a place by itself': one can picture a sort of empty turban, where the head of Jesus had rested. At once the women ran to fetch some other disciples: and it was when Peter himself entered the tomb, and stared in wonder at the empty grave-clothes, that 'he saw and believed'.

And when the sabbath was past, Mary Magdalene, and Mary the mother of James, and Salome, bought spices, so that they might go and anoint him. And very early on the first day of the week they went to the tomb when the sun had risen. And they were saying to one another, 'Who will roll away the stone for us from the door of the tomb?' And looking up, they saw that the stone was rolled back; for it was very large. And entering the tomb, they saw a young man sitting on the right side, dressed in a white robe; and they were amazed. And he said to them, 'Do not be amazed; you seek Jesus of Nazareth, who was crucified. He has risen, he is not here; see the place where they laid him. But go, tell his disciples and Peter that he is going before you to Galilee; there you will see him, as he told you.' And they went out and fled from the tomb; for trembling and astonishment had come upon them; and they said nothing to any one, for they were afraid.

MARK 16:1-8 *RSV*

68

'THE LORD HAS RISEN!'

In the accounts we have of Jesus after his
resurrection, he is clearly the same and yet not the
same: his resurrection body is one with his earthly
body, but changed — what the New Testament
calls 'glorified'. These two disciples (man and wife,
some have thought) are preoccupied, lost in their
thoughts and discussions. Only afterwards did
they realize that this was no ordinary companion
on the road.

Now that same day two of them were going
to a village called Emmaus, about seven miles
from Jerusalem. They were talking with each
other about everything that had happened. As
they talked and discussed these things with
each other, Jesus himself came up and walked
along with them; but they were kept from
recognising him.

He asked them, 'What are you discussing
together as you walk along?'

They stood still, their faces downcast. One
of them, named Cleopas, asked him, 'Are you
only a visitor to Jerusalem and do not know the
things that have happened there in these days?'

'What things?' he asked.

'About Jesus of Nazareth,' they replied. 'He
was a prophet, powerful in word and deed
before God and all the people. The chief priests
and our rulers handed him over to be sentenced
to death, and they crucified him; but we had
hoped that he was the one who was going to
redeem Israel. And what is more, it is the third
day since all this took place. In addition, some of
our women amazed us. They went to the tomb
early this morning but didn't find his body. They
came and told us that they had seen a vision of
angels, who said he was alive. Then some of
our companions went to the tomb and found
it just as the women had said, but him they
did not see.'

He said to them, 'How foolish you are,
and how slow of heart to believe all that the
prophets have spoken! Did not the Christ have
to suffer these things and then enter his glory?'
And beginning with Moses and all the Prophets,
he explained to them what was said in all the
Scriptures concerning himself.

As they approached the village to which
they were going, Jesus acted as if he were going

further. But they urged him strongly, 'Stay with us, for it is nearly evening; the day is almost over.' So he went in to stay with them.

When he was at the table with them, he took bread, gave thanks, broke it and began to give it to them. Then their eyes were opened and they recognised him, and he disappeared from their sight. They asked each other, 'Were not our hearts burning within us while he talked with us on the road and opened the Scriptures to us?'

LUKE 24:13-32 *NIV*

69

IN GALILEE

'I am going fishing' says Peter to his friends — just what you might expect a fisherman to say. But there may be more to it than meets the eye. For three years now, Peter has been totally fulfilled; he has been one of Jesus' inner circle, always with him, travelling and teaching, marshalling the crowds, busy as the day is long. Then suddenly it is all ended — not only in the terrible memory of the crucifixion, but with the searing personal tragedy of Peter's desertion and betrayal. Peter had been a fisherman in these very waters before Jesus met and called him. Does not 'I'm going fishing' sound like a final return to the old life, with nothing left from these three years but bitter memories of his tragic denial?

Here at the lakeside, in the very early morning, Peter has a chance to put that right. On this familiar beach he will be recommissioned to serve Jesus. 'Peter, do you love me?' Jesus goes on to ask him, 'then feed my lambs, shepherd my sheep.'

Simon Peter, Thomas called the Twin, Nathanael of Cana in Galilee, the sons of Zebedee, and two others of his disciples were together. Simon Peter said to them, 'I am going fishing.' They said to him, 'We will go with you.' They went out and got into the boat; but that night they caught nothing.

Just as day was breaking, Jesus stood on the beach; yet the disciples did not know that it was Jesus. Jesus said to them, 'Children, have you any fish?' They answered him, 'No.' He said to them, 'Cast the net on the right side of the boat, and you will find some.' So they cast it, and now they were not able to haul it in, for the quantity of fish. That disciple whom Jesus loved said to Peter, 'It is the Lord!' When Simon Peter heard that it was the Lord, he put on his clothes, for he was stripped for work, and sprang into the sea. But the other disciples came in the boat, dragging the net full of fish, for they were not far from the land, but about a hundred yards off.

When they got out on land, they saw a charcoal fire there, with fish lying on it, and bread. Jesus said to them, 'Bring some of the fish that you have just caught.' So Simon Peter went aboard and hauled the net ashore, full of large fish, a hundred and fifty-three of them; and although there were so many, the net was not torn. Jesus said to them, 'Come and have breakfast.' Now none of the disciples dared ask him, 'Who are you?' They knew it was the Lord. Jesus came and took the bread and gave it to them, and so with the fish. This was now the third time that Jesus was revealed to the disciples after he was raised from the dead.

JOHN 21:2-14 *RSV*

70

'YOU ARE MY WITNESSES'

Jesus, in his resurrection body, appears to the disciples. To convince them that he is no mere ghost he allows them to touch him, and eats food before their eyes.

Yet again he turns them to the Old Testament Scriptures to help them understand the meaning behind these great events through which they have been living. Now their task is to tell what they know. In the power of God's promised gift, the Holy Spirit, it is for them, the eye-witnesses, to begin to share the good news.

And so, with a final blessing, Jesus is taken up into the heaven from which he came. You would expect to find on the faces of these eleven men signs of bewilderment and fear, grief and desolation. But no: though taken from them, Jesus is still with them always 'even to the end of time'. Because of that his followers knew then, as ever afterwards, a joy that the world cannot give nor take away.

As they were talking about all this, there Jesus was, standing among them. Startled and terrified, they thought they were seeing a ghost. But he said, 'Why are you so perturbed? Why do questionings arise in your minds? Look at my hands and feet. It is I myself. Touch me and see; no ghost has flesh and bones as you can see that I have.' They were still unconvinced, still wondering, for it seemed too good to be true. So he asked them, 'Have you anything here to eat?' They offered him a piece of fish they had cooked, which he took and ate before their eyes.

And he said to them, 'This is what I meant by saying, while I was still with you, that everything written about me in the Law of Moses and in the prophets and psalms was bound to be fulfilled.' Then he opened their minds to understand the scriptures. 'This,' he said, 'is what is written: that the Messiah is to suffer death and to rise from the dead on the third day, and that in his name repentance bringing the forgiveness of sins is to be proclaimed to all nations. Begin from Jerusalem; it is you who are the witnesses to it all. And mark this: I am sending upon you my Father's promised gift; so stay here in this city until you are armed with the power from above.'

Then he led them out as far as Bethany, and blessed them with uplifted hands; and in the act of blessing he parted from them. And they returned to Jerusalem with great joy, and spent all their time in the temple praising God.

LUKE 24:36-53 *NEB*

71

THE DAY OF PENTECOST

Men and women are made in the image of God. At the creation it was 'God's breath' that was breathed into them, so that 'man became a living soul'. Yet God's breath or Spirit, if not totally withdrawn, became less in evidence as the years passed. It was given at special times to special individuals (like the prophets), but it was no longer the dynamic, life-giving experience of the whole people of God, let alone the world around them.

But here at the start of Luke's account of the Acts of the apostles we are reminded by the apostle Peter of God's promise that a day would come when the Holy Spirit would again be widely poured out. Peter went on to proclaim that, in the wake of Christ's coming, and his death and resurrection, that long-awaited Day of the Lord is here.

When the day of Pentecost had come, they were all together in one place. And suddenly a sound came from heaven like the rush of a mighty wind, and it filled all the house where they were sitting. And there appeared to them tongues as of fire, distributed and resting on each one of them. And they were all filled with the Holy Spirit and began to speak in other tongues, as the Spirit gave them utterance.

Now there were dwelling in Jerusalem Jews, devout men from every nation under heaven. And at this sound the multitude came together, and they were bewildered, because each one heard them speaking in his own language. And they were amazed and wondered, saying, 'Are not all these who are speaking Galileans? And how is it that we hear, each of us in his own native language? Parthians and Medes and Elamites and residents of Mesopotamia, Judea and Cappadocia, Pontus and Asia, Phrygia and Pamphylia, Egypt and the parts of Libya belonging to Cyrene, and visitors from Rome, both Jews and proselytes, Cretans and Arabians, we hear them telling in our own tongues the mighty works of God.' And all were amazed and perplexed, saying to one another, 'What does this mean?' But others mocking said, 'They are filled with new wine.'

But Peter, standing with the eleven, lifted up his voice and addressed them, 'Men of Judea and all who dwell in Jerusalem, let this be known to you, and give ear to my words. For these men are not drunk, as you suppose, since it is only the third hour of the day; but this is what was spoken by the prophet Joel:

"And in the last days it shall be, God declares,
that I will pour out my Spirit upon all flesh,
and your sons and your daughters shall prophesy,
and your young men shall see visions,
and your old men shall dream dreams;
yea, and on my menservants and my maidservants
    in those days
I will pour out my Spirit; and they shall prophesy.
And I will show wonders in the heaven above
and signs on the earth beneath,
blood, and fire, and vapour of smoke;
the sun shall be turned into darkness
and the moon into blood,
before the day of the Lord comes,
the great and manifest day.
And it shall be that whoever calls on the name
    of the Lord shall be saved."

'Men of Israel, hear these words: Jesus of Nazareth, a man attested to you by God with mighty works and wonders and signs which God did through him in your midst, as you yourselves know — this Jesus, delivered up according to the definite plan and foreknowledge of God, you crucified and killed by the hands of lawless men. But God raised him up, having loosed the pangs of death, because it was not possible for him to be held by it.'

ACTS 2:1-24 *RSV*

72

THE FIRST BELIEVERS

Among Peter's hearers in Jerusalem were some of those who had shouted 'Crucify! Crucify!' on that first Good Friday. With stunning directness, they are now told by the Spirit-filled disciples that 'God has made him both Lord and Christ, this Jesus whom you crucified.' Deeply troubled at what they have done, the people question Peter as to how they can put themselves right with God. Peter's reply describes what is still happening every day, in all parts of the world, as men and women come in faith to Jesus Christ. Turning from sin and turning to Christ in faith and trust is the decisive movement of the heart, the crossing of the threshold of Christian discipleship. From it comes the fresh start, the forgiveness of our past sins, and the gift of God's Holy Spirit for the new life now beginning as a follower of Christ. With it goes the rite of baptism in his name, the outward and visible sign and seal of commitment to him.

Luke the historian gives us here a glimpse of the 'honeymoon period' of those first Christians. We see their sense of fellowship and joy as members of a new family, their hunger to learn, their growing spiritual appetite. The power of God is very close about them and his love flows out from them to others. Bitter persecution, even martyrdom, lies ahead of many of them; but for the moment they enjoy the respect of their community, and are seeing their friends and neighbours discovering for themselves that 'Christ is alive' and ready to receive them also into his fellowship.

When the people heard this, they were deeply troubled and said to Peter and the other apostles, 'What shall we do, brothers?'

Peter said to them, 'Each one of you must turn away from his sins and be baptized in the name of Jesus Christ, so that your sins will be forgiven; and you will receive God's gift, the Holy Spirit. For God's promise was made to you and your children, and to all who are far away — all whom the Lord our God calls to himself.'

Peter made his appeal to them and with many other words he urged them, saying, 'Save yourselves from the punishment coming on this wicked people!' Many of them believed his message and were baptized, and about three thousand people were added to the group that day. They spent their time in learning from the apostles, taking part in the fellowship, and sharing in the fellowship meals and the prayers.

Many miracles and wonders were being done through the apostles, and everyone was filled with awe. All the believers continued together in close fellowship and shared their belongings with one another. They would sell their property and possessions, and distribute the money among all, according to what each one needed. Day after day they met as a group in the Temple, and they had their meals together in their homes, eating with glad and humble hearts, praising God, and enjoying the good will of all the people. And every day the Lord added to their group those who were being saved.

ACTS 2:37-47 *GNB*

PHILIP AND THE ETHIOPIAN

Philip was among the seven men chosen as the first deacons or ministers of the church — and history knows him as 'Philip the Evangelist'. This story gives us a glimpse of him at this work, sharing with all who were ready to listen the good news of Jesus Christ.

Though Luke tells us that 'this road is not used nowadays', it was in Philip's day a busy trade route. Here, in the providence of God, Philip as evangelist meets a seeker after truth. This high official (we should call him a Chancellor of the Exchequer) had come from Jerusalem, the holy city. His mind would have been full of what he had seen, and before leaving he had bought for himself ('to read on the journey') a part of the Jewish Scriptures. As he reads Isaiah's prophecy of a Saviour who would be 'the Lamb of God', and die for the sins of the people, the Ethiopian asks Philip if he can explain the passage. Philip did not need asking twice. As the oxen lumbered steadily forward, 'he told him the Good News about Jesus'.

'Seek and you shall find,' Jesus had promised. To the hungry heart of this traveller, Jesus comes as all that he has been seeking. On that dusty road, by some wayside pool, he turns his heart to Christ, is baptized into his new faith, and begins to experience the joy of the believer.

An angel of the Lord said to Philip, 'Get ready and go south to the road that goes from Jerusalem to Gaza.' (This road is not used nowadays.) So Philip got ready and went. Now an Ethiopian eunuch, who was an important official in charge of the treasury of the queen of Ethiopia, was on his way home. He had been to Jerusalem to worship God and was going back home in his carriage. As he rode along, he was reading from the book of the prophet Isaiah. The Holy Spirit said to Philip, 'Go over to that carriage and stay close to it.' Philip ran over and heard him reading from the book of the prophet Isaiah. He asked him, 'Do you understand what you are reading?'

The official replied, 'How can I understand unless someone explains it to me?' And he invited Philip to climb up and sit in the carriage with him. The passage of scripture which he was reading was this:

'Like a sheep that is taken to be
        slaughtered,
    like a lamb that makes no sound when its
        wool is cut off,
    he did not say a word.

He was humiliated, and justice was
        denied him.
No one will be able to tell about his
        descendants,
    because his life on earth has come to an end.'

The official asked Philip, 'Tell me, of whom is the prophet saying this? Of himself or of someone else?' Then Philip began to speak; starting from this passage of scripture, he told him the Good News about Jesus. As they travelled down the road, they came to a place where there was some water, and the official said, 'Here is some water. What is to keep me from being baptized?'

The official ordered the carriage to stop, and both Philip and the official went down into the water, and Philip baptized him. When they came up out of the water, the Spirit of the Lord took Philip away. The official did not see him again, but continued on his way, full of joy.

ACTS 8:26-39 *GNB*

BROTHER SAUL

This has been called the story, not of a sudden conversion, but of a sudden surrender. It begins a long way back, perhaps at that moment when the men stoning to death the first Christian martyr, Stephen, 'laid down their coats at the feet of a young man called Saul'.

Saul, a distinguished Pharisee, had set himself to suppress this new heretical religion as a threat to the historic faith of Judaism. It became an obsession with him. Not content with persecuting Christians where he found them, he began to seek them out. His name was a byword among the early church, a name of terror.

From Jerusalem to Damascus was a week's journey. We can picture Saul walking the dusty road day after day in great turmoil of spirit, perhaps unsure of himself or his mission, uncertain where truth lay. And so God draws near to him. Saul's world is turned upside-down. He surrenders to the living God whom he has been vainly trying to evade. And in Damascus, welcomed (who knows with what misgivings) by the little Christian community, he is baptized and filled with the Holy Spirit, and begins courageously to preach and teach that Jesus is the Son of God.

Meanwhile, Saul was still breathing out murderous threats against the Lord's disciples. He went to the high priest and asked him for letters to the synagogues in Damascus, so that if he found any there who belonged to the Way, whether men or women, he might take them as prisoners to Jerusalem. As he neared Damascus on his journey, suddenly a light from heaven flashed around him. He fell to the ground and heard a voice say to him, 'Saul, Saul, why do you persecute me?'

'Who are you, Lord?' Saul asked.

'I am Jesus, whom you are persecuting,' he replied. 'Now get up and go into the city, and you will be told what you must do.'

The men travelling with Saul stood there speechless; they heard the sound but did not see anyone. Saul got up from the ground, but when he opened his eyes he could see nothing. So they led him by the hand into Damascus. For three days he was blind, and did not eat or drink anything.

In Damascus there was a disciple named Ananias. The Lord called to him in a vision, 'Ananias!'

'Yes, Lord,' he answered.

The Lord told him, 'Go to the house of Judas on Straight Street and ask for a man from Tarsus

named Saul, for he is praying. In a vision he has seen a man named Ananias come and place his hands on him to restore his sight.'

'Lord,' Ananias answered, 'I have heard many reports about this man and all the harm he has done to your saints in Jerusalem. And he has come here with authority from the chief priests to arrest all who call on your name.'

But the Lord said to Ananias, 'Go! This man is my chosen instrument to carry my name before the Gentiles and their kings and before the people of Israel. I will show him how much he must suffer for my name.'

Then Ananias went to the house and entered it. Placing his hands on Saul, he said, 'Brother Saul, the Lord — Jesus, who appeared to you on the road as you were coming here — has sent me so that you may see again and be filled with the Holy Spirit.' Immediately, something like scales fell from Saul's eyes, and he could see again. He got up and was baptized, and after taking some food, he regained his strength.

ACTS 9:1-19 *NIV*

AT PHILIPPI IN PRISON

Paul and Silas are on a missionary journey, spreading the faith as they travel from town to town. Paul made three such major journeys, with different companions at different times. Philippi was a city with immense civic pride, and at this time a Roman colony. In the course of their ministry there Paul and Silas healed a slave-girl who was spirit-possessed and used by her owners to tell fortunes. These men, furious at the loss of income her deliverance would mean for them, dragged Paul and Silas before the magistrates, and the city was soon in a riot. Paul and Silas were cruelly beaten, and flung into the innermost prison with their feet in the stocks.

About midnight, Luke tells us, Paul and Silas felt a tremor and then a shaking. As the earthquake took hold, the whole prison began to collapse about them, the doors swung open, the very fetters became unfastened.

This Philippian jailer is yet another man in whose heart God has been preparing the way of Christ. His world has fallen about his ears; in the dust and darkness he has been a moment away from suicide; he needs help and he knows it. And to his question 'What must I do to be saved?' (with the emphasis surely on the 'I' — 'What about *me*? What must *I* do . . ?') Paul returns the classic answer of the New Testament. In the small hours, they instruct him in the faith. He cares for their needs and hangs upon their words. Presently he and his whole family are baptized. And so the church grows.

About midnight Paul and Silas, at their prayers, were singing praises to God, and the other prisoners were listening, when suddenly there was such a violent earthquake that the foundations of the jail were shaken; all the doors burst open and all the prisoners found their fetters unfastened. The jailer woke up to see the prison doors wide open, and assuming that the prisoners had escaped, drew his sword intending to kill himself. But Paul shouted, 'Do yourself no harm; we are all here.' The jailer called for lights, rushed in and threw himself down before Paul and Silas, trembling with fear. He then escorted them out and said, 'Masters, what must I do to be saved?' They said, 'Put your trust in the Lord Jesus, and you will be saved, you and your household.' Then they spoke the word of the Lord to him and to everyone in his house. At that late hour of the night he took them and washed their wounds; and immediately afterwards he and his whole family were baptized. He brought them into his house, set out a meal, and rejoiced with his whole household in his new-found faith in God.

ACTS 16:25-34 *NEB*

'TO AN UNKNOWN GOD'

Athens remains, even today, a legendary city. It was famous in Paul's day for its great university, its temples, statues and monuments. It represented 'the glory that was Greece' — but a glory given over, in the eyes of the apostle, to superstition and idolatry.

Among these Athenians, full of intellectual speculation and enquiry, Paul makes his famous speech to 'the Council of the Areopagus', a prestigious gathering of civic leaders. Starting from an inscription many of them would pass daily in the city, and quoting from their own literature, Paul speaks to them about the true knowledge of God. He tells them of God as Creator, Spirit, Life-giver, and as the Sustainer of all he has made. Yet he is also a God of love, caring for men and women as his children, drawing near to them as he reveals himself to them and they respond.

Paul then goes on to preach about the sinfulness of men, and their need for repentance before a God of holiness and judgment. He is clearly preparing the ground for a full presentation of the divine person and saving work of Christ.

As always, the gospel divides. To the proud Athenian spirit of intellectual analysis, this talk of resurrection from the dead is ludicrous. But among some hearers, the seed of life is patiently being sown.

Paul stood before the whole Council of the Areopagus and made this speech:

'Men of Athens, I have seen for myself how extremely scrupulous you are in all religious matters, because I noticed, as I strolled around admiring your sacred monuments, that you had an altar inscribed: To An Unknown God. Well, the God whom I proclaim is in fact the one whom you already worship without knowing it.

'Since the God who made the world and everything in it is himself Lord of heaven and earth, he does not make his home in shrines made by human hands. Nor is he dependent on anything that human hands can do for him, since he can never be in need of anything; on the contrary, it is he who gives everything — including life and breath — to everyone. From one single stock he not only created the whole human race so that they could occupy the entire earth, but he decreed how long each nation should flourish and what the boundaries of its territory should be. And he did this so that all nations might seek the deity and, by feeling their way towards him, succeed in finding him. Yet in fact he is not far from any of us, since it is in him that we live, and move, and exist, as indeed some of your own writers have said:

"We are all his children."

'Since we are the children of God, we have no excuse for thinking that the deity looks like anything in gold, silver or stone that has been carved and designed by a man.

'God overlooked that sort of thing when men were ignorant, but now he is telling everyone everywhere that they must repent, because he has fixed a day when the whole world will be judged, and judged in righteousness, and he has appointed a man to be the judge. And God has publicly proved this by raising this man from the dead.'

At this mention of rising from the dead, some of them burst out laughing; others said, 'We would like to hear you talk about this again.'

ACTS 17:22-32 JB

PAUL'S FAREWELL TO EPHESUS

Paul is on his way to Jerusalem and breaks his journey at Miletus, the port for Ephesus. The Ephesian church was very dear to him. As he reminds the leaders who came to meet him, he had spent three years among them, earning his living as a tent-maker, and using every opportunity to teach the faith and found a Christian church.

He reminds them also of the two great themes which appear all through the New Testament and which formed the basis of his preaching: repentance before a holy God, and faith in Jesus Christ as the one who can forgive sins. Now, he tells them, the spiritual responsibility is theirs. He has done his part. They are to shepherd the flock of Christ in their community.

Paul is well aware that in Jerusalem he may face arrest and trial. So the apostle and his converts kneel and pray together for the last time, and make their sad farewells before his ship sets sail. But Paul leaves them in the knowledge that his work among them has established a church full of life and vigour, with a mature Christian leadership trained and ready to meet whatever the future may hold for them.

'Take heed to yourselves and to all the flock, in which the Holy Spirit has made you guardians, to feed the church of the Lord which he obtained with his own blood. I know that after my departure fierce wolves will come in among you, not sparing the flock; and from among your own selves will arise men speaking perverse things, to draw away the disciples after them. Therefore be alert, remembering that for three years I did not cease night or day to admonish every one with tears. And now I commend you to God and to the word of his grace, which is able to build you up and to give you the inheritance among all those who are sanctified. I coveted no one's silver or gold or apparel. You yourselves know that these hands ministered to my necessities, and to those who were with me. In all things I have shown you that by so toiling one must help the weak, remembering the words of the Lord Jesus, how he said, "It is more blessed to give than to receive."'

And when he had spoken thus, he knelt down and prayed with them all. And they all wept and embraced Paul and kissed him, sorrowing most of all because of the word he had spoken, that they should see his face no more. And they brought him to the ship.

ACTS 20:28-37 *RSV*

78

PAUL BEFORE AGRIPPA

Among the Jews, Paul's preaching continued to be a storm-centre. Plots were hatched against his life, and he was taken into protective custody by the Roman authorities. Rather than stand trial locally for the accusations made against him, he exercised the right of every Roman citizen with the words 'I appeal to Caesar'.

But while waiting for a ship to take him to Rome, Paul had the opportunity to explain his position not only to Festus, the Roman provincial governor, but also to his guest Agrippa, puppet-king of a small local kingdom.

So Paul tells again the story of his conversion to Christ, and the work to which God had first called him on that Damascus road. 'I stand here as a witness' says Paul, as he must have said time and again in so many of the cities of Asia; and he skilfully offers to Festus and Agrippa and the whole assembly the heart of his preaching: to repent of sin, to turn to God, and to live the new life of obedience to Christ. And because Agrippa would be well-versed in the Jewish faith he shows how the story of Jesus, crucified and risen, fulfils the whole thrust of the Jewish Scriptures from Moses to the Prophets.

'The fact that I lived from my youth upwards among my own people in Jerusalem is well known to all Jews. They have known all the time, and could witness to the fact if they wished, that I lived as a Pharisee according to the strictest sect of our religion. Even today I stand here on trial because of a hope that I hold in a promise that God made to our forefathers — a promise for which our twelve tribes serve God zealously day and night, hoping to see it fulfilled. It is about this hope, your majesty, that I am being accused by Jews! Why does it seem incredible to you all that God should raise the dead? I once thought it my duty to oppose with the utmost vigour the name of Jesus of Nazareth. Yes, that is what I did in Jerusalem, and I had many of God's people imprisoned on the authority of the chief priests, and when they were on trial for their lives I gave my vote against them. Many and many a time in all the synagogues I had them punished and I used to try and force them to deny their Lord. I was mad with fury against them, and I hounded them to distant cities. Once, your majesty, on my way to Damascus on this business, armed with the full authority and commission of the chief priests, at midday I saw a light from Heaven, far brighter than the sun, blazing about me and my fellow-travellers. We all fell to the ground and I heard a voice saying to me in Hebrew, 'Saul, Saul, why are you persecuting me? It is not easy for you to kick against your own conscience.' 'Who are you, Lord?' I said. And the Lord said to me, 'I am Jesus whom you are persecuting. Now get up and stand on your feet for I have shown myself to you for a reason — you are chosen to be my servant and a witness of what you have seen of me today, and of other visions of myself which I will give you. I will keep you safe both from your own people and from the gentiles to whom I now send you. I send you to open their eyes, to turn them from darkness to light, from the power of Satan to God himself, so that they may know forgiveness of their sins and take their place with all those who are made holy by their faith in me.' After that, King Agrippa, I could not disobey the heavenly vision. But both in Damascus and in Jerusalem, through the whole of Judaea, and to the gentiles, I preached that men should repent and turn to God and live lives to prove their change of heart. This is why the Jews seized me in the Temple and tried to kill me. To this day I have received help from God himself, and I stand here as a witness to high and low, adding nothing to what the prophets and Moses foretold should take place, that is, that Christ should suffer, that he should be the first to rise from the dead, and so proclaim the message of light both to our people and to the gentiles!'

ACTS 26:4-23 *JBP*

79

PAUL IN ROME

This is the last glimpse we have of Paul. Here in Rome, at the centre of the known world, the hub of a great network of Roman roads and communications, he lived under house-arrest and continued with undiminished energies and zeal to commend Christ. He began, as always, with his own people, the Jewish community.

But though his message was for the Jews, it was not for them alone. His call is to present the claims of Christ to Jew and Gentile alike. So in the last verse of his two-volume history, Luke speaks of him welcoming 'all who came to him', and explaining to them the good news of Jesus.

Meanwhile he carried on an altogether wider ministry. From this house-arrest sprang many pastoral letters, some of which we read today in our New Testament as Holy Scripture, God's living word to his church in every age.

When we entered Rome Paul was allowed to lodge by himself with a soldier in charge of him. Three days later he called together the local Jewish leaders; and when they were assembled, he said to them: 'My brothers, I, who never did anything against our people or the customs of our forefathers, am here as a prisoner; I was handed over to the Romans at Jerusalem. They examined me and would have liked to release me because there was no capital charge against me; but the Jews objected, and I had no option but to appeal to the Emperor; not that I had any accusation to bring against my own people. That is why I have asked to see you and talk to you, because it is for the sake of the hope of Israel that I am in chains, as you see'. They replied, 'We have had no communication from Judaea, nor has any countryman of ours arrived with any report or gossip to your discredit. We should like to hear from you what your views are; all we know about this sect is that no one has a good word to say for it.'

So they fixed a day, and came in large numbers as his guests. He dealt at length with the whole matter; he spoke urgently of the kingdom of God and sought to convince them about Jesus by appealing to the Law of Moses and the prophets. This went on from dawn to dusk. Some were won over by his arguments; others remained sceptical.

ACTS 28:16-24 *NEB*

NO CONDEMNATION . . . NO SEPARATION

Paul's letter to the Christians at Rome was written in advance of his visit to them, and includes the fullest and most detailed statement of his Christian world-view and the good news of Jesus as he expounded it. In this celebrated chapter he reaches the triumphant conclusion of his arguments with words of liberation and hope. Those who are committed to Christ, God's Son, our Saviour, are freed and forgiven. The bondage of the Jewish system of law, with its impossible demands, is broken for ever. The sins of the past find forgiveness through the cross of Christ where he became our sin-offering, dying in our place, and given for us all.

And Christ not only died for us, but is raised to life and seated in power at God's right hand. His love is over us, regardless of circumstances. There lies our final security. If our trust is in the God of love, we can face the future with total confidence.

Therefore, there is now no condemnation for those who are in Christ Jesus, because through Christ Jesus the law of the Spirit of life set me free from the law of sin and death. For what the law was powerless to do in that it was weakened by the sinful nature, God did by sending his own Son in the likeness of sinful man to be a sin offering . . .

If God is for us, who can be against us? He who did not spare his own Son, but gave him up for us all — how will he not also, along with him, graciously give us all things? Who will bring any charge against those whom God has chosen? It is God who justifies. Who is he that condemns? Christ Jesus, who died — more than that, who was raised to life — is at the right hand of God and is also interceding for us. Who shall separate us from the love of Christ? Shall trouble or hardship or persecution or famine or nakedness or danger or sword? As it is written:

'For your sake we face death all day long; we are considered as sheep to be slaughtered.'

No, in all these things we are more than conquerors through him who loved us. For I am convinced that neither death nor life, neither angels nor demons, neither the present nor the future, nor any powers, neither height nor depth, nor anything else in all creation, will be able to separate us from the love of God that is in Christ Jesus our Lord.

ROMANS 8:1-3,31-39 *NIV*

81

CHRISTIAN LIVING

When in 1947 J.B. Phillips published his free translation of the New Testament epistles under the title *Letters to Young Churches*, the phrase 'Don't let the world around you squeeze you into its own mould . . .' soon became a much-quoted example of the vitality of the New Testament message for today. In a striking passage in the introduction, J.B. Phillips compared himself to an electrician re-wiring an ancient house without being able to 'turn the mains off'.

In these verses, still very much 'alive' and full of meaning for us today, Paul speaks of true worship as rooted in daily Christian living — and of how Christian living is an entirely practical affair, transforming our relationships with one another, and helping us to say 'Yes' to life.

With eyes wide open to the mercies of God, I beg you, my brothers, as an act of intelligent worship, to give him your bodies, as a living sacrifice, consecrated to him and acceptable by him. Don't let the world around you squeeze you into its own mould, but let God re-mould your minds from within, so that you may prove in practice that the plan of God for you is good, meets all his demands and moves towards the goal of true maturity . . .

Let us have no imitation Christian love. Let us have a genuine break with evil and a real devotion to good. Let us have real warm affection for one another as between brothers, and a willingness to let the other man have the credit. Let us not allow slackness to spoil our work and let us keep the fires of the spirit burning, as we do our work for God. Base your happiness on your hope in Christ. When trials come endure them patiently; steadfastly maintain the habit of prayer. Give freely to fellow-Christians in want, never grudging a meal or a bed to those who need them. And as for those who try to make your life a misery, bless them. Don't curse, bless. Share the happiness of those who are happy, and the sorrow of those who are sad. Live in harmony with each other. Don't become snobbish but take a real interest in ordinary people. Don't become set in your own opinions. Don't pay back a bad turn by a bad turn, to *anyone*. Don't say 'it doesn't matter what people think', but see that your public behaviour is above criticism. As far as your responsibility goes, live at peace with everyone. Never take vengeance into your own hands, my dear friends: stand back and let God punish if he will. For it is written:

'Vengeance belongeth unto me:
I will recompense.'

And these are God's words:

'If thine enemy hunger, feed him;
If he thirst, give him to drink:
For in so doing thou shalt heap
coals of fire upon his head.'

Don't allow yourself to be overpowered with evil. Take the offensive — overpower evil by good!

ROMANS 12:1-2,9-21 *JBP*

82

THE MESSAGE OF THE CROSS

At the heart of Paul's message, as at the heart of the Bible, is the cross of Christ. But in his day as in ours there was a 'foolishness' about the cross. People asked then as they ask now, 'How can one man's death so long ago make the smallest difference to me? I feel no need of a Saviour: I can manage very well for myself, thank you.' There are still plenty, like the Jews Paul describes, who say 'Let God prove himself to me, and then I will believe'; or who want, like the Greeks, an intellectual gospel.

But Paul (a better Jew than most, and with a scholar's mind and training) had no other gospel to offer. His message was Jesus Christ, through whose death alone forgiveness and deliverance can be found. And because of this, faith does not depend on learning, or on great powers of understanding. The wise and the simple, the great and the humble — all are equal at the foot of the cross.

For the message about Christ's death on the cross is nonsense to those who are being lost; but for us who are being saved it is God's power. The scripture says,

'I will destroy the wisdom of the wise and set aside the understanding of the scholars.'

So then, where does that leave the wise? or the scholars? or the skilful debaters of this world? God has shown that this world's wisdom is foolishness!

For God in his wisdom made it impossible for people to know him by means of their own wisdom. Instead, by means of the so-called 'foolish' message we preach, God decided to save those who believe. Jews want miracles for proof, and Greeks look for wisdom. As for us, we proclaim the crucified Christ, a message that is offensive to the Jews and nonsense to the Gentiles; but for those whom God has called, both Jews and Gentiles, this message is Christ, who is the power of God and the wisdom of God. For what seems to be God's foolishness is wiser than human wisdom, and what seems to be God's weakness is stronger than human strength.

I CORINTHIANS 1:18-25 *GNB*

84

THE GREATEST OF THESE ...

If there are 'golden oldies' in Bible translation, this is such a passage, and for that reason the time-honoured version is given here. Read aloud, it is incomparable in the beauty of its language.

'Charity' in this famous passage is simply 'love'. Every modern translation uses the word 'love'; and there is no difficulty in reading these words from the Authorized Version, changing the word *charity* (at least in our minds) into *love* each time Paul uses it.

But Paul was not writing just for the beauty of the words. He was describing the life that is ruled by love — and which has only ever perfectly been seen in the earthly life of Jesus.

83

'IN REMEMBRANCE OF ME'

Paul was not one of the first apostles like Peter, James or John. He never met or followed Jesus as they did in Judea and Galilee. But it was Paul's claim that the risen and ascended Christ had appeared to him in a personal way, and that Jesus himself had been his teacher and instructor, as he was of the original twelve apostles.

Here he is reminding the Christians at Corinth of how Jesus instituted his memorial supper; and that those of every generation who share that supper in obedience to Christ are both remembering and proclaiming his death for them.

The teaching I gave you was given me personally by the Lord himself, and it was this: the Lord Jesus, in the same night in which he was betrayed, took bread and when he had given thanks he broke it and said, 'Take, eat, this is my body which is being broken for you. Do this in remembrance of me.' Similarly, when supper was ended, he took the cup saying, 'This cup is the new agreement in my blood: do this, whenever you drink it, in remembrance of me.'

This can only mean that whenever you eat this bread or drink of this cup, you are proclaiming that the Lord has died for you, and you will do that until he comes again. So that, whoever eats the bread or drinks the wine without due thought is making himself like one of those who allowed the Lord to be put to death without discerning who he was.

No, a man should thoroughly examine himself, and only then should he eat the bread or drink of the cup. He that eats and drinks carelessly is eating and drinking a judgment on himself, for he is blind to the presence of the Lord's body.

I CORINTHIANS 11:23-29 *JBP*

Though I speak with the tongues of men and of angels, and have not charity, I am become as sounding brass, or a tinkling cymbal. And though I have the gift of prophecy, and understand all mysteries, and all knowledge; and though I have all faith, so that I could remove mountains, and have not charity, I am nothing. And though I bestow all my goods to feed the poor, and though I give my body to be burned, and have not charity, it profiteth me nothing. Charity suffereth long, and is kind; charity envieth not; charity vaunteth not itself, is not puffed up, Doth not behave itself unseemly, seeketh not her own, is not easily provoked, thinketh no evil; Rejoiceth not in iniquity, but rejoiceth in the truth; Beareth all things, believeth all things, hopeth all things, endureth all things. Charity never faileth; but whether there be prophecies, they shall fail; whether there be tongues, they shall cease; whether there be knowledge, it shall vanish away. For we know in part, and we prophesy in part. But when that which is perfect is come, then that which is in part shall be done away. When I was a child, I spake as a child, I understood as a child, I thought as a child; but when I became a man, I put away childish things. For now we see through a glass, darkly; but then face to face: now I know in part; but then shall I know even as also I am known. And now abideth faith, hope, charity, these three; but the greatest of these is charity.

I CORINTHIANS 13:1-13 KJV

85

LIFE OUT OF DEATH

The life to come will always seem mysterious. There must be elements of it which, even if they could be perfectly explained to us, we could not at present understand. But we are all familiar with one kind of 'resurrection of the body' already, when we sow seeds in the earth. In the life beyond the grave which God promises to each believer, we shall still be ourselves, but changed into a resurrection body fitted for the life of heaven.

Meanwhile, death is still 'the last enemy'. Yet for the Christian, its days are numbered and its sting is drawn. Death, for all its human sadness of parting, cannot finally defeat us. In his Easter resurrection, Christ has won the victory. The day is coming when Christ's followers will share the life of eternity with him, and death will be no more.

But someone may ask, 'How are the dead raised? With what kind of body will they come?' How foolish! What you sow does not come to life unless it dies. When you sow, you do not plant the body that will be, but just a seed, perhaps of wheat or of something else. But God gives it a body as he has determined, and to each kind of seed he gives its own body. All flesh is not the same: Men have one kind of flesh, animals have another, birds another and fish another. There are also heavenly bodies and there are earthly bodies; but the splendour of the heavenly bodies is one kind, and the splendour of the earthly bodies is another. The sun has one kind of splendour, the moon another and the stars another; and star differs from star in splendour.

So will it be with the resurrection of the dead. The body that is sown is perishable, it is raised imperishable; it is sown in dishonour, it is raised in glory; it is sown in weakness, it is raised in power; it is sown a natural body, it is raised a spiritual body . . .

Listen, I tell you a mystery: We will not all sleep, but we will all be changed — in a flash, in the twinkling of an eye, at the last trumpet. For the trumpet will sound, the dead will be raised imperishable, and we will be changed. For the perishable must clothe itself with the imperishable, and the mortal with immortality. When the perishable has been clothed with the imperishable, and the mortal with immortality, then the saying that is written will come true:

'Death has been swallowed up in victory.'

'Where, O death, is your victory?
Where, O death, is your sting?'

The sting of death is sin, and the power of sin is the law. But thanks be to God! He gives us the victory through our Lord Jesus Christ.

I CORINTHIANS 15:35-44,51-57 *NIV*

GOD'S GIFT

William Temple, Archbishop of Canterbury in the 1940s, used to say that there was nothing any of us could contribute towards our redemption, except the sin from which we needed to be redeemed. Here in this passage it is brought home to us that we are saved by grace, by God's undeserved favour towards us, in the gift of his Son, through faith. Faith is the empty hand stretched out to receive what God offers.

There is no way in which we can earn salvation — not by our prayers, or good works, or generosity or sacrifice. Salvation is God's gift.

The 'life of good deeds' comes afterwards. It is the result of salvation, not its cause.

In the past you were spiritually dead because of your disobedience and sins. At that time you followed the world's evil way; you obeyed the ruler of the spiritual powers in space, the spirit who now controls the people who disobey God. Actually all of us were like them and lived according to our natural desires, doing whatever suited the wishes of our own bodies and minds. In our natural condition we, like everyone else, were destined to suffer God's anger.

But God's mercy is so abundant, and his love for us is so great, that while we were spiritually dead in our disobedience he brought us to life with Christ. It is by God's grace that you have been saved. In our union with Christ Jesus he raised us up with him to rule with him in the heavenly world. He did this to demonstrate for all time to come the extraordinary greatness of his grace in the love he showed us in Christ Jesus. For it is by God's grace that you have been saved through faith. It is not the result of your own efforts, but God's gift, so that no one can boast about it. God has made us what we are, and in our union with Christ Jesus he has created us for a life of good deeds, which he has already prepared for us to do.

EPHESIANS 2:1-10 *GNB*

87

THE ARMOUR OF GOD

Paul probably wrote this letter to the church at Ephesus (a church, as we have seen, that had a particular place in his affections) from his house-arrest at Rome. There, in the company of a Roman soldier day and night, he would have been as familiar with the uniform as he was with his own clothes.

It was very natural, therefore, that in picturing the Christian well-prepared for the spiritual battle, he should draw on the imagery of the 'armour of God'. It has reminded Christians ever since that the call to follow Christ is the call to fight his battles.

Finally, be strong in the Lord and in the strength of his might. Put on the whole armour of God, that you may be able to stand against the wiles of the devil. For we are not contending against flesh and blood, but against the principalities, against the powers, against the world rulers of this present darkness, against the spiritual hosts of wickedness in the heavenly places. Therefore take the whole armour of God, that you may be able to withstand in the evil day, and having done all, to stand. Stand therefore, having girded your loins with truth, and having put on the breastplate of righteousness, and having shod your feet with the equipment of the gospel of peace; above all taking the shield of faith, with which you can quench all the flaming darts of the evil one. And take the helmet of salvation, and the sword of the Spirit, which is the word of God.

EPHESIANS 6:10-17 *RSV*

88

AT THE NAME OF JESUS . . .

One way to learn about human nature is to watch very young children. Along with their interest in one another, there is often a revealing self-centredness. Who has not heard at a children's party the cry 'Me first!'?

It is the exact opposite of the way of Jesus. He came from the power and glory of his home in heaven, and (in the words of an earlier translation) 'emptied himself'; or, as here 'humbled himself', 'made himself nothing'. The death that he accepted for our sakes was the death of a common criminal on a Roman gallows.

So, says Paul, what about those who claim to follow him? For Christ's followers it cannot be 'me first'. The days of rivalry and vanity and envy must be left behind.

And as for Jesus who humbled himself, God 'raised him to the heights'. The name that was despised by so many of his fellow-countrymen is now above all names. Jesus Christ the crucified is 'Jesus Christ the Lord'.

If then our common life in Christ yields anything to stir the heart, any loving consolation, any sharing of the Spirit, any warmth of affection or compassion, fill up my cup of happiness by thinking and feeling alike, with the same love for one another, the same turn of mind, and a common care for unity. There must be no room for rivalry and personal vanity among you, but you must humbly reckon others better than yourselves. Look to each other's interest and not merely to your own.

Let your bearing towards one another arise out of your life in Christ Jesus. For the divine nature was his from the first; yet he did not think to snatch at equality with God, but made himself nothing, assuming the nature of a slave. Bearing the human likeness, revealed in human shape, he humbled himself, and in obedience accepted even death — death on a cross. Therefore God raised him to the heights and bestowed on him the name above all names, that at the name of Jesus every knee should bow — in heaven, on earth, and in the depths — and every tongue confess, 'Jesus Christ is Lord', to the glory of God the Father.

PHILIPPIANS 2:1-11 *NEB*

A MIND AT EASE

'It's all in the mind' we say sometimes. A sense of inferiority or anxiety, the confidence to achieve, depression or well-being — 'it's all in the mind'.

So Paul tells the Christians at Philippi some of the secrets of a mind at ease. Its thoughts will turn often towards Christ and his blessings. It will rejoice with thanksgiving and praise. God's care can put to rest all human anxieties and his peace can drive away worries and evil thoughts.

But more than this, the Christian mind should be turned towards what is good and true. A habit of thinking and cast of mind go far to determine the people that we are.

Rejoice in the Lord always. I will say it again: Rejoice! Let your gentleness be evident to all. The Lord is near. Do not be anxious about anything, but in everything, by prayer and petition, with thanksgiving, present your requests to God. And the peace of God, which transcends all understanding, will guard your hearts and your minds in Christ Jesus.

Finally, brothers, whatever is true, whatever is noble, whatever is right, whatever is pure, whatever is lovely, whatever is admirable — if anything is excellent or praiseworthy — think about such things. Whatever you have learned or received or heard from me, or seen in me — put it into practice. And the God of peace will be with you.

PHILIPPIANS 4:4-9 *NIV*

90

THE DEAD IN CHRIST

The New Testament contains many references to the fact of Christ's return in glory. The Christian creeds affirm that Christ, risen and ascended, 'shall come again with glory to judge both the quick (that is, the living) and the dead'. This passage gives us some glimpses, a vision seen through earthly eyes, of that final Day of the Lord. It is the fullest description in the New Testament, and yet offers the barest outline. Our concern is not with the when or how of Christ's return, but of who it is that comes — 'the Lord himself will come down from heaven'.

Paul writes here to set at rest anxieties that had arisen in the church at Thessalonica about the Christian dead. Would they miss the Lord's return? Would they be somehow at a disadvantage? No, Paul tells them. When the trumpet sounds for that great day the dead and the living will be reunited and 'with the Lord for ever'.

We want you to be quite certain, brothers, about those who have died, to make sure that you do not grieve about them, like the other people who have no hope. We believe that Jesus died and rose again, and that it will be the same for those who have died in Jesus: God will bring them with him. We can tell you this from the Lord's own teaching, that any of us who are left alive until the Lord's coming will not have any advantage over those who have died. At the trumpet of God, the voice of the archangel will call out the command and the Lord himself will come down from heaven; those who have died in Christ will be the first to rise, and then those of us who are still alive will be taken up in the clouds, together with them, to meet the Lord in the air. So we shall stay with the Lord for ever. With such thoughts as these you should comfort one another.

1 THESSALONIANS 4:13-18 *JB*

91

A GOOD SOLDIER

Timothy was Paul's 'son in the faith', probably a convert won to Christ through Paul's ministry at Lystra, Timothy's home town. He was clearly young in years for the spiritual leadership that was asked of him, and of a timid disposition; but his loyalty to Paul was met by a particular affection and concern, shown in the two pastoral letters addressed to him by name which form part of the New Testament.

Here Paul is urging timid Timothy to stand firm for the gospel, and to be willing to pay the price of suffering, arduous training, and sheer hard work. He is to 'Remember Jesus . . .', and also to have in mind the sufferings of the apostle himself, probably in Rome.

You then, my son, be strong in the grace that is in Christ Jesus, and what you have heard from me before many witnesses entrust to faithful men who will be able to teach others also. Take your share of suffering as a good soldier of Christ Jesus. No soldier on service gets entangled in civilian pursuits, since his aim is to satisfy the one who enlisted him. An athlete is not crowned unless he competes according to the rules. It is the hard-working farmer who ought to have the first share of the crops. Think over what I say, for the Lord will grant you understanding in everything.

Remember Jesus Christ, risen from the dead, descended from David, as preached in my gospel, the gospel for which I am suffering and wearing fetters, like a criminal. But the word of God is not fettered. Therefore I endure everything for the sake of the elect, that they also may obtain the salvation which in Christ Jesus goes with eternal glory. The saying is sure:

If we have died with him, we shall also live
    with him;
if we endure, we shall also reign with him;
if we deny him, he also will deny us;
if we are faithless, he remains faithful —
for he cannot deny himself.

Remind them of this, and charge them before the Lord to avoid disputing about words, which does no good, but only ruins the hearers. Do your best to present yourself to God as one approved, a workman who has no need to be ashamed, rightly handling the word of truth.

2 TIMOTHY 2:1-15 *RSV*

92

GOD'S FINAL WORD

Sometimes when we need to be in touch with friends we telephone, or send a letter. For a special occasion we may send flowers. But there are particular moments when there is no substitute for meeting face to face, being there in person. 'I came myself', we say.

Here the writer is explaining that God has sent many messengers to his people, one after another down the centuries. But now he has come himself, in the person of Jesus Christ, his Son. Language however eloquent, or prophets however inspired, are no longer enough. We see God most clearly when we see him in a person — and that person his divine Son, 'the exact representation of his being'. If we want to know what God is like, as best we can understand him, we must look long and hard at Jesus Christ.

Angels are God's messengers, but it was not an angel God sent to us. The rest of the chapter makes it clear that angels are God's creatures — his servants. Jesus is his Son.

In the past God spoke to our forefathers through the prophets at many times and in various ways, but in these last days he has spoken to us by his Son, whom he appointed heir of all things, and through whom he made the universe. The Son is the radiance of God's glory and the exact representation of his being, sustaining all things by his powerful word. After he had provided purification for sins, he sat down at the right hand of the Majesty in heaven. So he became as much superior to the angels as the name he has inherited is superior to theirs.

HEBREWS 1:1-4 *NIV*

93

THE UNTAMEABLE TONGUE

The letter of James is full of practical down-to-earth teaching about Christian behaviour. Here he reminds us how easily our tongue trips us up, and how difficult it is to control the sins of speech. If the phrase 'vast potentialities for evil' seems too exaggerated, think of the harm that is done by the lie, the slander, the sarcastic word. It is small wonder that the instruction not to bear false witness should find a place among the ten commandments.

Sometimes people pride themselves on their bluntness and directness of speech — never mind who gets hurt; or alternatively on their tact and diplomacy, even if it does mean 'a little white lie'. The Christian needs to have the balance right, following the example of Jesus himself. He was described as 'full of grace and truth' — not one without the other, but both in harmony.

We all make mistakes in all kinds of ways, but the man who can claim that he never says the wrong thing can consider himself perfect, for if he can control his tongue he can control every other part of his personality! Men control the movements of a large animal like the horse with a tiny bit placed in its mouth. Ships too, for all their size and the momentum they have with a strong wind behind them, are controlled by a very small rudder according to the course chosen by the helmsman. The human tongue is physically small, but what tremendous effects it can boast of! A whole forest can be set ablaze by a tiny spark of fire, and the tongue is as dangerous as any fire, with vast potentialities for evil. It can poison the whole body, it can make the whole of life a blazing hell.

Beasts, birds, reptiles and all kinds of sea-creatures can be, and in fact are, tamed by man, but no one can tame the human tongue. It is an evil always liable to break out, and the poison it spreads is deadly. We use the tongue to bless our Father, God, and we use the same tongue to curse our fellow-men, who are all created in God's likeness. Blessing and curses come out of the same mouth — surely, my brothers, this is the sort of thing that never ought to happen! Have you ever known a spring to give sweet and bitter water simultaneously? Have you ever seen a fig-tree with a crop of olives, or seen figs growing on a vine? It is just as impossible for a spring to give fresh and salt water at the same time.

JAMES 3:2-12 *JBP*

94

CHRIST'S SUFFERINGS AND OURS

In this letter the apostle Peter has a word for Christians in different situations — for wives and husbands, for the leaders of the church family, and for its younger members; and here for those who are household servants. In writing to them about their circumstances, he gives us all an unforgettable picture of Christ as the one who suffered for us.

Peter reminds these servants (who were often slaves, blamed and punished for faults they had not committed) that Jesus is their example; but to say no more than that is to say too little. Christ is also the Saviour of the world. His death makes possible the forgiveness of sins.

You servants must submit to your masters and show them complete respect, not only to those who are kind and considerate, but also to those who are harsh. God will bless you for this, if you endure the pain of undeserved suffering because you are conscious of his will. For what credit is there if you endure the beatings you deserve for having done wrong? But if you endure suffering even when you have done right, God will bless you for it. It was to this that God called you, for Christ himself suffered for you and left you an example, so that you would follow in his steps. He committed no sin, and no one ever heard a

95

TENDING THE FLOCK

Peter, who began as a fisherman for Christ, was re-commissioned after Jesus' resurrection with the words 'Feed my lambs, tend my sheep'. Here he writes to the elders or pastors of the local churches where his letter would be read aloud, urging them to take pains over their shepherding, to set an example, to give themselves to the care of Christ's flock.

The younger members of the church, he tells them, must for their part be humble enough to receive such guidance — and all alike must be on guard. In this life Christians must expect their share of suffering — 'brief suffering' Peter calls it — but God is in control; his followers are in his keeping; and he calls them to share at last in his eternal glory.

And now I appeal to the elders of your community, as a fellow-elder and a witness of Christ's sufferings, and also a partaker in the splendour that is to be revealed. Tend that flock of God whose shepherds you are, and do it, not under compulsion, but of your own free will, as God would have it; not for gain but out of sheer devotion; not tyrannizing over those who are allotted to your care, but setting an example to the flock. And then, when the Head Shepherd appears, you will receive for your own the unfading garland of glory.

In the same way you younger men must be subordinate to your elders. Indeed, all of you should wrap yourselves in the garment of humility towards each other, because God sets his face against the arrogant but favours the lie come from his lips. When he was insulted, he did not answer back with an insult; when he suffered, he did not threaten, but placed his hopes in God, the righteous Judge. Christ himself carried our sins in his body to the cross, so that we might die to sin and live for righteousness. It is by his wounds that you have been healed. You were like sheep that had lost their way, but now you have been brought back to follow the Shepherd and Keeper of your souls.

I PETER 2:18-25 *GNB*

humble. Humble yourselves then under God's mighty hand, and he will lift you up in due time. Cast all your cares on him, for you are his charge.

Awake! be on the alert! Your enemy the devil, like a roaring lion, prowls round looking for someone to devour. Stand up to him, firm in faith, and remember that your brother Christians are going through the same kinds of suffering while they are in the world. And the God of all grace, who called you into his eternal glory in Christ, will himself, after your brief suffering, restore, establish, and strengthen you on a firm foundation. He holds dominion for ever and ever. Amen.

I PETER 5:1-11 *NEB*

John writes in this letter to Christians who are worried by the problem of their sins. When they first turned to Christ in repentance and faith, they claimed his promise that their sins were forgiven. They passed from darkness to light. They began to lead the new life, walking in the light of God's presence with them.

But, while we are in this world, we have not done with sin. Sometimes believers slip and fall and are ashamed. John tells his readers that God does not reject those who fall into sin — but that 'if we confess our sins . . . he will forgive.' So the Christian can get up and go on, walking in the light, and learning the lessons of failure. By Christ's sacrifice for sins, the past is left behind, and the believer is clean again. God is not only light but love.

God is light; in him there is no darkness at all. If we claim to have fellowship with him yet walk in the darkness, we lie and do not live by the truth. But if we walk in the light, as he is in the light, we have fellowship with one another, and the blood of Jesus, his Son, purifies us from all sin.

If we claim to be without sin, we deceive ourselves and the truth is not in us. If we confess our sins, he is faithful and just and will forgive us our sins and purify us from all unrighteousness.

I JOHN 1:5-9 *NIV*

JOHN ON PATMOS

The last book of the Bible is called the Revelation of St John. It consists of a series of visions and prophecies given to the aged apostle when he was in exile on the island of Patmos, fifty miles off the coast of Turkey — in John's day, part of the Roman province of Asia. It is written in a style and literary form known as *apocalyptic*, more familiar in John's day than in ours.

One Sunday John was given this vision of 'one like a son of man', coupled with a command to write down what he saw and send it to the churches of the mainland. These seven churches are represented by golden lampstands (they are

to shed the light of Christ upon their local communities), while the angels may refer to the church leaders, or to some heavenly guardian appointed to each of the churches to stand watch over its life.

The vision is of Christ in glory 'alive for evermore', having taken possession of the keys of death and hell so that he can release their prisoners and destroy their power. He is 'the first and the last', from eternity to eternity. John's ecstatic vision represents the dignity and majesty, the power and victory, of the crucified and risen Christ.

I was in the Spirit on the Lord's day, and I heard behind me a loud voice like a trumpet saying, 'Write what you see in a book and send it to the seven churches, to Ephesus and to Smyrna and to Pergamum and to Thyatira and to Sardis and to Philadelphia and to Laodicea.'

Then I turned to see the voice that was speaking to me, and on turning I saw seven golden lampstands, and in the midst of the lampstands one like a son of man, clothed with a long robe and with a golden girdle round his breast; his head and his hair were white as white wool, white as snow; his eyes were like a flame of fire, his feet were like burnished bronze, refined as in a furnace, and his voice was like the sound of many waters; in his right hand he held seven stars, from his mouth issued a sharp two-edged sword, and his face was like the sun shining in full strength.

When I saw him, I fell at his feet as though dead. But he laid his right hand upon me, saying, 'Fear not, I am the first and the last, and the living one; I died, and behold I am alive for evermore, and I have the keys of Death and Hades. Now write what you see, what is and what is to take place hereafter. As for the mystery of the seven stars which you saw in my right hand, and the seven golden

lampstands, the seven stars are the angels of the seven churches and the seven lampstands are the seven churches.

REVELATION 1:10-20 *RSV*

98

A LUKEWARM CHURCH

John is not only to share his vision of Christ with the churches of Asia; but for each of them the Spirit gives to him an individual and appropriate message from Christ himself.

Laodicea was the last of these seven churches. Others had been sent their special letters on the theme of love or suffering, holiness or opportunity. To the Christians at Laodicea the challenge is to their wholeheartedness — whether they are earnest in their discipleship.

They think of themselves as rich (their city was a financial centre for the region) — but they are blind and naked in the poverty of their love for Christ. And what does their Master ask of them now? Just what he had preached to so many in his earthly ministry — repentance and faith. Let them recognize their true condition and open their hearts to Christ by faith. At Laodicea, he is kept waiting on the doorstep; but his true place must be as the head of the household, the centre of the Christian's life.

'These are the words of the Amen, the faithful and true witness, the beginning of God's creation:

I know what you have done, and that you are neither cold nor hot. I could wish that you were either cold or hot! But since you are lukewarm and neither hot nor cold, I intend to spit you out of my mouth! While you say, "I am rich, I have prospered, and there is nothing that I need," you have no eyes to see that you are wretched, pitiable, poverty-stricken, blind and naked. My advice to you is to buy from me that gold which is purified in the furnace so that you may be rich, and white garments to wear so that you may hide the shame of your nakedness, and salve to put on your eyes to make you see. All those whom I love I correct and discipline. Therefore, shake off your complacency and repent. See, I stand knocking at the door. If anyone listens to my voice and opens the door, I will go into his house and dine with him, and he with me. As for the victorious, I will give him the honour of sitting beside me on my throne, just as I myself have won the victory and have taken my seat beside my Father on his throne. Let the listener hear what the Spirit says to the Churches.'

REVELATION 3:14-22 *JBP*

99

GLORY TO THE LAMB!

Jesus is the Lamb of God — the sacrificial victim, to whom all the Old Testament sacrifices look forward; but with this difference, that his was both a willing and a perfect sacrifice. He is the Lamb of God who takes away the sin of the world; and here in John's great vision of heaven he is the Lamb victorious and enthroned.

Before him in the courts of heaven there stands an innumerable company from every tribe and race, who have found forgiveness of their sins and new life in Christ. That is what is meant by the expression 'washed their robes and made them white in the blood of the Lamb'. The words 'the blood' in the Bible point always to Christ's death, his blood shed for sinners. And by his death his people are made clean from all their past sins, and covered with the robe of Christ's perfect righteousness.

So for a moment, we catch a glimpse of heaven. God reigns, and Christ shares his throne. Death and suffering are past and done with. Hunger and thirst, all our unsatisfied longings, are quenched for ever in the perpetual springs of the water of eternal life.

After this I looked and saw a vast throng, which no one could count, from every nation, of all tribes, peoples, and languages, standing in front of the throne and before the Lamb. They were robed in white and had palms in their hands, and they shouted together:

'Victory to our God who sits on the throne, and to the Lamb!'

And all the angels stood round the throne and the elders and the four living creatures, and they fell on their faces before the throne and worshipped God, crying:

'Amen! Praise and glory and wisdom, thanksgiving and honour, power and might, be to our God for ever and ever! Amen.'

Then one of the elders turned to me and said, 'These men that are robed in white — who are they and from where do they come?' But I answered, 'My lord, you know, not I.' Then he said to me, 'These are the men who have passed through the great ordeal; they have washed their robes and made them white in the blood of the Lamb. That is why they stand before the throne of God and minister to him day and night in his temple; and he who sits on the throne will dwell with them. They shall never again feel hunger or thirst, the sun shall not beat on them nor any scorching heat, because the Lamb who is at the heart of the throne will be their shepherd and will guide them to the springs of the water of life; and God will wipe all tears from their eyes.'

REVELATION 7:9-17 *NEB*

100

THE HOLY CITY

The name Jerusalem means 'the city of peace'. For centuries it had been for the Jewish nation a symbol of their spiritual home and of divine blessing. Torn by war and destruction, its very temple desecrated and demolished, it was still the City of God.

Now, in John's vision, we see why. There is to be at the end of the age 'a new Jerusalem', a true holy city, in the new heaven and the new earth that God has in store for those who love him. Inklings of this new age run through the pages of the New Testament but here John offers a dramatic vision symbolizing all that is to be.

The language is poetic, the picture figurative and visionary; like the climax of a mighty symphony, it speaks to us where words and meanings fail.

But it is not an imaginary vision. Behind the symbol stands a far greater reality, unimaginable and inconceivable in its richness and splendour to earthbound creatures of space and time. At the heart of John's prophetic vision lies this clear assurance, that in God's heavenly city his people will know and enjoy him for ever in the light and glory of Christ, and of God's new and everlasting day.

Then I saw a new heaven and a new earth; for the first heaven and the first earth had passed away, and the sea was no more. And I saw the holy city, new Jerusalem, coming down out of heaven from God, prepared as a bride adorned for her husband; and I heard a great voice from the throne saying, 'Behold, the dwelling of God is with men. He will dwell with them, and they shall be his people and God himself will be with them; he will wipe away every tear from their eyes, and death shall be no more, neither shall there be mourning nor crying nor pain any more, for the former things have passed away.'

And he who sat upon the throne said, 'Behold, I make all things new.' Also he said, 'Write this, for these words are trustworthy and true.' And he said to me, 'It is done! I am the Alpha and Omega, the beginning and the end. To the thirsty I will give water without price from the fountain of the water of life. He who conquers shall have this heritage, and I will be his God and he shall be my son.'

And I saw no temple in the city, for its temple is the Lord God the Almighty and the Lamb. And the city has no need of sun or moon to shine upon it, for the glory of God is its light, and its lamp is the Lamb. By its light shall the nations walk; and the kings of the earth shall bring their glory into it, and its gates shall never be shut by day — and there shall be no night there; they shall bring into it the glory and the honour of the nations. But nothing unclean shall enter it, nor any one who practises abomination or falsehood, but only those who are written in the Lamb's book of life.

REVELATION 21:1-7,22-27 *RSV*